LEOPOLDO LUGONES
Selected Writings

$ .00

LEOPOLDO LUGONES
Selected Writings

Translated from the Spanish by
SERGIO WAISMAN

Edited with an Introduction by
GWEN KIRKPATRICK

OXFORD
UNIVERSITY PRESS

2008

OXFORD
UNIVERSITY PRESS

Oxford University Press, Inc., publishes works that further
Oxford University's objective of excellence
in research, scholarship, and education.

Oxford   New York
Auckland   Cape Town   Dar es Salaam   Hong Kong   Karachi
Kuala Lumpur   Madrid   Melbourne   Mexico City   Nairobi
New Delhi   Shanghai   Taipei   Toronto

With offices in
Argentina   Austria   Brazil   Chile   Czech Republic   France   Greece
Guatemala   Hungary   Italy   Japan   Poland   Portugal   Singapore
South Korea   Switzerland   Thailand   Turkey   Ukraine   Vietnam

Copyright © 2008 by Oxford University Press, Inc.

Published by Oxford University Press, Inc.
198 Madison Avenue, New York, New York 10016

www.oup.com

Oxford is a registered trademark of Oxford University Press

Library of Congress Cataloging-in-Publication Data
Lugones, Leopoldo, 1874–1938.
[Selections. English. 2007]
Leopoldo Lugones : selected writings / translated from the Spanish
by Sergio Waisman ; edited with an introduction by Gwen Kirkpatrick.
p.   cm.
Includes bibliographical references.
ISBN 978-0-19-517405-2; 978-0-19-517404-5 (pbk.)
1.   Lugones, Leopoldo, 1874–1938.—Translations into English.
I.   Waisman, Sergio, Gabriel.
II.   Kirkpatrick, Gwen.   III.   Title.
PQ7797. L85A2 2007
868'.6208—dc22   2007035818

1 3 5 7 9 8 6 4 2

Printed in the United States of America
on acid-free paper

Contents

Series Editors'
General Introduction

The Library of Latin America series makes available in translation major nineteenth-century authors whose work has been neglected in the English-speaking world. The titles for the translations from the Spanish and Portuguese were suggested by an editorial committee that included Jean Franco (general editor responsible for works in Spanish), Richard Graham (series editor responsible for works in Portuguese), Tulio Halperín Donghi (at the University of California, Berkeley), Iván Jaksić (at the Pontificia Universidad Católica de Chile), Naomi Lindstrom (at the University of Texas at Austin), and Francine Masiello (at the University of California, Berkeley). The late Eduardo Lozano of the Library at the University of Pittsburgh and the late Antonio Cornejo Polar of the University of California, Berkeley, were also founding members of the committee. The translations have been funded thanks to the generosity of the Lampadia Foundation and the Andrew W. Mellon Foundation.

During the period of national formation between 1810 and the early years of the twentieth century, the new nations of Latin America fashioned their identities, drew up constitutions, engaged in bitter struggles over territory, and debated questions of education, government, ethnicity, and culture. This was a unique period unlike that during the process of nation formation in Europe and one that should be more familiar than it is to students of comparative politics, history, and literature.

The image of the nation was envisioned by the lettered classes—a minority in countries in which indigenous, mestizo, black, or mulatto peasants and slaves predominated—although there were also alternative nationalisms at the grassroots level. The cultural elite were well educated in European thought and letters, but as statesmen, journalists, poets, and academics, they confronted the problem of the racial and linguistic heterogeneity of the continent and the difficulties of integrating the population into a modern nation-state. Some of the writers whose works will be translated in the Library of Latin America series played leading roles in politics. Fray Servando Teresa de Mier, a friar who translated Rousseau's *The Social Contract* and was one of the most colorful characters of the independence period, was faced with imprisonment and expulsion from Mexico for his heterodox beliefs; on his return, after independence, he was elected to the congress. Domingo Faustino Sarmiento, exiled from his native Argentina under the dictatorship of Rosas, wrote *Facundo: Civilización y barbarie*, a stinging denunciation of that government. He returned after Rosas's overthrow and was elected president in 1868. Andrés Bello was born in Venezuela, lived in London, where he published poetry during the independence period, and settled in Chile, where he founded the university, wrote his grammar of the Spanish language, and drew up the country's legal code.

These post-independence intelligentsia were not simply dreaming castles in the air but vitally contributing to the founding of nations and the shaping of culture. The advantage of hindsight may make us aware of problems they themselves did not foresee, but this should not affect our assessment of their truly astonishing energies and achievements. Although there is a recent translation of Sarmiento's celebrated *Facundo*, there is no translation of his memoirs, *Recuerdos de provincia* (*Provincial Recollections*). The predominance of memoirs in the Library of Latin America Series is no accident—many of these offer entertaining insights into a vast and complex continent.

Nor have we neglected the novel. The series includes new translations of the outstanding Brazilian writer Machado de Assis's work, including *Dom Casmurro* and *The Posthumous Memoirs of Brás Cubas*. There is no reason why other novels that are not so well known outside Latin America—the Peruvian novelist Clorinda Matto de Turner's *Aves sin nido*, Nataniel Aguirre's *Juan de la Rosa*, José de Alencar's *Iracema*, Juana Manuela Gorriti's short stories—should not be read with as much interest as the political novels of Anthony Trollope.

A series on nineteenth-century Latin America cannot, however, be limited to literary genres such as the novel, the poem, and the short story. The literature of independent Latin America was eclectic and strongly influenced by the periodical press newly liberated from scrutiny by colonial authorities and the Inquisition. Newspapers were miscellanies of fiction, essays, poems, and translations from all manner of European writing. The novels written on the eve of Mexican independence by José Joaquín Fernández de Lizardi included disquisitions on secular education and law, and denunciations of the evils of gaming and idleness. Other works, such as a well-known poem by Andrés Bello, "Ode to Tropical Agriculture," and novels such as *Amalia* by José Mármol and the Bolivian Nataniel Aguirre's *Juan de la Rosa*, were openly partisan. By the end of the century, sophisticated scholars were beginning to address the history of their countries, as did João Capistrano de Abreu in his *Capítulos de história colonial*.

It is often in memoirs such as those by Fray Servando Teresa de Mier or Sarmiento that we find the descriptions of everyday life that in Europe were incorporated into the realist novel. Latin American literature at this time was seen largely as a pedagogical tool, a "light" alternative to speeches, sermons, and philosophical tracts—though, in fact, especially in the early part of the century, even the readership for novels was quite small because of the high rate of illiteracy. Nevertheless the vigorous orally transmitted culture of the gaucho and the urban underclasses became the linguistic repertoire of some of the most interesting nineteenth-century writers—most notably José Hernández, author of the "gauchesque" poem "Martín Fierro," which enjoyed an unparalleled popularity. But for many writers the task was not to appropriate popular language but to civilize, and their literary works were strongly influenced by the high style of political oratory.

The editorial committee has not attempted to limit its selection to the better-known writers such as Machado de Assis; it has also selected many works that have never appeared in translation and writers whose works have not been translated recently. The series now makes these works available to the English-speaking public.

Because of the preferences of funding organizations, the series initially focuses on writing from Brazil, the Southern Cone, the Andean region, and Mexico. Each of our editions will have an introduction that places the work in its appropriate context and includes explanatory notes.

We owe special thanks to the late Robert Glynn of the Lampadia Foundation, whose initiative gave the project a jump start, and to Richard Ekman and his successors at the Andrew W. Mellon Foundation, which also generously supported the project. We also thank the Rockefeller Foundation for funding the 1996 symposium "Culture and Nation in Iberoamerica," organized by the editorial board of the Library of Latin America. The support of Edward Barry of Oxford University Press was crucial in the founding years of the project, as have been the advice and help of Ellen Chodosh and Elda Rotor of Oxford University Press. The John Carter Brown Library at Brown University in Providence, Rhode Island, has been serving since 1998 as the grant administrator of the project.

—Jean Franco
—Richard Graham

Introduction

Leopoldo Lugones (1874–1938), a man of extraordinary talents and a decidedly mixed legacy in both literature and politics, is generally credited as the initiator of the fantastic short story in Latin America, a forerunner to the masters of the form, Horacio Quiroga, Julio Cortázar, and Jorge Luis Borges. As a poet, with his innovative *Lunario sentimental* (1909), he definitively changed the tone and form of poetry in Spanish, paving the way for the avant-garde. During his life he was heralded as the foremost man of Argentine letters, as poet, short story writer, essayist, historian, philologist, and political thinker. His vast writings range from experimental poetry to biography to gaucho tales and to the exploration of classicism, science, and the occult. In *El payador* (1916) he canonized the verse epic *Martín Fierro* (1872, 1879) by José Hernández as the mythic foundation of the nation. For Lugones, this work, like the classical epics, elevated the values of the vast pampas, just as Argentina paradoxically was becoming a nation largely of urban immigrants. In this gesture, as in so many others, he moved against the grain of history, yet he attracted many who yearned for stability of institutions, language, and society, even at the price of repression.

In politics, he began his career as a socialist and ended it as a fascist, a defender of the "hour of the sword," a phrase he used in the infamous speech "The Ayacucho Address," included in this volume. Delivered in 1924, this speech would forever cloud his remarkable literary legacy. Although he never held a high government office, his support of the antidemocratic Uriburu's overthrow of populist president Yrigoyen in 1930 sealed his reputation as an ally of military repression. His increasingly vehement proclamations, as well as a fascination with Mussolini, tainted both his political and literary reputations. His suicide in 1938, shortly after that of fellow writer Horacio Quiroga,[1] further complicated his literary and political legacy and fueled speculation on his own sense of his legacy.[2] Did he see himself as the upholder of tradition unjustly reviled by the new generation? Or did he judge himself on the torturous paths he had taken? Borges explains his death simply as a decision to avoid scandal, an illicit love affair gone bad, yet it is tempting to see this moment on a larger scale, as many of his critics have done.

In any attempt to understand Argentine intellectual history, Lugones is a force to be reckoned with; his presence appears almost to haunt his successors, even Jorge Luis Borges, who pays him an ambivalent homage in his dedication to Lugones of *El otro, el mismo* and who also published a book-length essay on Lugones in the 1950s. In an interview near the end of his life, Borges names Lugones as the initiator of the fantastic short story in Latin America: "Happily for our America and for the Spanish language, Lugones published in 1905 [*sic*] *Strange Forces*, a book of deliberately fantastic stories. And Lugones is usually forgotten and it is thought that our generation . . . well, let's say Bioy Casares, Silvina Ocampo and I, initiated that type of literature that propagated and produced writers as illustrious as García Márquez or Cortázar."[3] But Borges as a younger man had joined his vanguardist contemporaries of the twenties in their scornful rejection of what Lugones stood for, seeing him as a pillar of bourgeois values and traditionalism in literature. Contemporary Argentine writers, such as Ricardo Piglia in *Artificial Respiration*, have echoed this rejection, calling him the "Buster Keaton of our culture."[4] Caricatured in periodicals almost from the time of his debut as a writer, Lugones evoked both admiration and disdain. Even Rubén Darío, who celebrated his entrance into letters and praised his work, noted the extremism and excess not only in his metaphors but also of his energetic convictions. On reviewing his first volume of poetry, *Las montañas del oro* (1898), Darío compared him to a young suitor eager to make an impression on his beloved: "If most men would bring a bouquet of flowers, Lugones would deliver the whole bush." Lugones was a prodigious self-taught intellect and wanted to make his mark not only as a writer but as a public voice. In contrast to the enmeshed roles of the writer and statesman of earlier times, the move of a writer into the political sphere in the early twentieth century was not a natural transition. As traced by numerous observers, most eloquently by Angel Rama in *The Lettered City*, the roles of writer and statesman began to move apart in the early twentieth century. No longer guaranteed a public forum on a large scale, the writer was increasingly relegated to a service position, particularly in journalism. While earlier figures such as Andrés Bello and Domingo Faustino Sarmiento could combine the roles of statesman and writer, marginalization was the path for most writers, starting with Lugones's generation.

We can trace the contradictory impulses of Lugones, his populist positions that hardened into exclusionary fascism, within the context of a rapidly changing Argentina. (Yet as we will see later on, these stances are not the most reliable tools for judging his literary works, for his fiction and poetry reveal struggles of the human subject that can lie outside public pronouncements.) He grew up near the country's most conservative and Catholic city, Córdoba, and as a young man set off to make his mark in Buenos Aires. Gradually he tempered his initial enthusiasm for cosmopolitan Buenos Aires, rejecting its massive immigration that brought a sure promise of the dislocation of traditional society. His ideas on literature, specifically on language itself, increasingly became tangled up with his ideas on the nation. Whereas earlier he had espoused the complete liberty of the artist (influenced by the Romantic view of the artist and profoundly by Nietzsche), he later developed theses on the morality of art, combining them with his extensive writings on classical literature and the sciences. In a peculiar judgment for a writer of fiction and poetry, he stated that inexact expression is equivalent to a lie, and therefore damaging to the public (*La nación*, Sept. 22, 1935).

Born in Villa de María in the province of Córdoba, Lugones began his career in the provincial capital city, Córdoba, publishing in local venues. From a family of modest means, he did not have a university career but did distinguish himself early on for his publications and public speeches.

In 1893 he cofounded, with Nicolás González Luján, a socialist and anticlerical periodical *El pensamiento libre* (Free Thought) and a socialist center, and he published poetry, initially under the pseudonym "Gil Paz." In 1897 he moved to Buenos Aires, a dynamic and modernizing city due to its vast immigration and an expanding economy. He quickly became part of the city's most influential socialist writers' group, including José Ingenieros and Roberto Payró, and began writing in the socialist journals *La vanguardia* and *La tribuna.* Even more decisively, he became friends with the Nicaraguan poet Rubén Darío, indisputably the literary leader of his and following generations, whose 1888 publication of *Azul* had revolutionized literature in Spanish. Darío facilitated for Lugones writing assignments in the major newspaper, *La nación.* Like Darío and most other writers of his generation, Lugones continued to work at more mundane jobs (for example, at the post office) to support his writing.[5] In 1898 he published his first book of poetry, *Las montañas del oro*, earning him an acclaimed place in the *modernistas*, the innovative group led by Darío. Darío praised Lugones's *modernity* in his remarks of 1896: "He is one of the 'moderns,' he is part of 'Young America.' . . . He follows the banners [of the new continent] because he has the temperament of a pure artist, his violent and vibrant spirit and his evident and invincible vocation."[6] Poetry was indeed a vocation for Lugones, and his later books of poetry, including the groundbreaking *Lunario sentimental* of 1909, have found readers throughout the Spanish-speaking world. Octavio Paz has attributed to Darío and to Lugones the two directions in modern poetry in Spanish: "*Cantos de vida y esperanza* [Darío 1905] and *Lunario sentimental* [1909] are the two major works of the second *modernismo*, and from them come, directly or indirectly, all the experiences and attempts of poetry in the Spanish language."[7] With *Lunario* Lugones was the first in Spanish to experiment with free verse, although he retained rhyme in all his poetry; the *Lunario*'s satiric, often shocking metaphors, directed at Western love's most revered symbols, unhinged the framework of lyricism in Spanish. Technical brilliance and irreverent experimentation inspired poets throughout the Spanish-speaking world, including poets as different as Peru's César Vallejo and Mexico's Ramón López Velarde. Yet in this volume, as in most of Lugones's poetry, the quality is uneven. Extraordinary poems like "White Solitude" coexist with hackneyed expressions. Despite his achievements as a poet, for later generations Lugones's image is inextricably linked to his role in the foundations of the modern short story and to his turbulent and often contradictory political positions.

In late nineteenth-century Buenos Aires, Lugones plunged into the heady intellectual life of a city rapidly undergoing the change from a hierarchical society dominated by the landowning classes to the origins of a new, predominantly urban middle class and the beginnings of democratization.[8] Intellectuals such as Lugones saw themselves as the vanguard of a new era, proponents of radical change and conduits of new truths from science, literature, philosophy, and the emerging social sciences into a society that needed intellectual guidance. Lugones attracted attention with his often bombastic proclamations, such as this one from 1899. "I understood, then, that America demanded a bitter mission: a mission of justice, and I decided to be, within the means of my power, above all and beyond all, the man who speaks the truth. . . . I stated that America did nothing to rid itself of its virginal ignorance; that we lived off imitation and foolish idolatry, fishing in a small boat like Simon of the biblical fable; that our literary storms were nothing more than small-voiced Saracens amongst dictionary cockroaches and Bohemian mosquitoes, and that all these problems would be resolved only when art stopped being a pretext and became a cause, when applause could be measured by merit and not by mutual interests."[9] At twenty-five, Lugones already exhibited the zealotry and polemic tone, as well as the odd animalistic detail, that would become sharper in later years. A disdain for some of his contemporaries was mixed with a lament for the "virginal ignorance" of America itself, a recasting of Sarmiento's classic pairing of "Civilization and Barbarism" from *Facundo*, the 1845 biography of a gaucho *caudillo* that sets forth the prescription of European civilization for an untamed Argentina. (Lugones wrote a biography of Sarmiento in 1910.)

For Lugones, radicalism among the intellectual elite was inevitable, and he actively promoted socialist and anarchist ideas in the nineties, combining them at times with ideas as varied as those of Darwin and Nietzsche. Book reviews, public addresses, and a series of caricatures of politicians served as fora for expounding his ideas on redemptive socialism. Three selections in this volume, "This Country's Politicians," "The Morality of Art," and "The Holiday of the Proletariat," are good examples of his mordant satire and the fiery rhetoric of the period. In his early years, he described a mythic *el pueblo* (the people) in a series of magnificent analogies as "the Lion," "eternal martyr," "immense collaborator with the Infinite," among other resounding phrases. His remarks are not out of place at the moment, for there was great activity among workers' movements,

especially since half the population of Buenos Aires was foreign born and included socialist and anarchist activists who
brought their organizing zeal from Italy and Spain. Critics
have debated the exact nature of his early socialism, some
regarding it as more of an aesthetic position than a political
one. Nonetheless, in his youth he was an active organizer
and an effective orator and writer for a mixture of political stances. Almost every reference to the "pueblo" includes
another indispensable factor, that of the "genius" or prophet
who can lead the people, a topic clearly figured in his first
book of poetry, where it coexists with a nocturnal, sexually
charged, and violent universe. Combining notions of the
Romantic genius and Nietzschean superman, Lugones first
expounded his ideas about an intellectual aristocracy as
early as 1894 in a flattering speech on the visit of the Duke
of Savoy to Buenos Aires. Needless to say, such pronouncements unsettled his socialist colleagues, but ideological
consistency was not an absolute requisite for the turbulent
times. As his politics moved steadily to the right, by 1916,
in the preface to *El payador* (the book of lectures on *Martín
Fierro*), he found the rural tradition as the source of the true
voice of the people, and the urban voices were denigrated
as the "foreign rabble" and the "majority breed," created by
the "lust of universal suffrage."[10] "On Immigration" (1930)
in this volume presents a more focused version of his later
ideas.

Like most intellectuals of his generation in Latin America, Lugones first viewed Spain, its Catholic tradition, and
its literature as oppressive traditions to be cast off in favor
of new currents from French, English, Italian, German,
and U.S. traditions. Much of his own journalism was devoted to introducing his readers to new writers, an eclec-

tic mix of European as well as contemporary Argentine and Latin American writers. In an early periodical he co-founded with the psychiatrist José Ingenieros, *La montaña: Periódico socialista revolucionario* (1897), the mix of articles is decidedly eclectic: they included notes on European and Latin American writers; articles on historical materialism, animism, and the union and socialist movements under-way in Europe, Bulgaria, China, Japan, and Brazil; poems and fiction by foreign writers (some in French or Italian not translated) like Tolstoy, Verlaine, and Ada Negri; and an ongoing scathing series by Ingenieros, "Bourgeois Reptiles,"[11] that earned a threat of censorship and fines from the mayor's office. In this journal, as in other early writings, the mix of topics and genres is disconcerting—poems, short stories, sketches, articles on philosophy, spiritism, science, politics, criminality, and art, among others. This eclecticism surely reflects his trying out different styles and topics, but it reflects as well the ferment of his epoch. Baudelaire had characterized the "modern" by its fleeting and changing na-ture, and even in what Beatriz Sarlo has called Argentina's "peripheral modernity," no one could escape the influx of information from multiple sources. And a writer like Lu-gones, hurrying to meet newspaper deadlines and job obli-gations, was not always able or willing to be selective. Yet as his friend Darío wrote to him, the newspaper business was a good laboratory for developing agility as a writer.[12]

Lugones was formed in the matrix of what is called *mod-ernismo* in Spanish America, a literary movement most closely associated with Rubén Darío; Buenos Aires and Mexico City were the two centers of its activity. "Moderni-sta" was first used derisively by more traditional critics, then proudly adopted by the new generation to label the literary innovations of these end-of-century writers (the movement is generally assigned to the period from 1888, the publication of Darío's *Azul*, to his death in 1916). Heavily influenced by symbolist currents in France and by striking rhythmic, lexical, and formal innovations, this variegated movement was best known for its poetry, often tinged with decadent or bohemian themes. Led by Darío, its poets, Cuba's José Martí and Julián del Casal, Colombia's José Asunción Silva, Mexico's Manuel Gutiérrez Nájera, Bolivia's Ricardo Jaimes Freire, Uruguay's Julio Herrera y Reissig and Delmira Agustini, among many others, made a clear break with what they perceived as a deadened and lifeless tradition in Spanish. In reaching primarily toward France, they sought a kind of literary decolonization, an independence from a Spain-dominated literary tradition.

While *modernista* poetry has received the most attention from later readers, prose forms were perhaps as important in shaping a new literature for Latin America. As Aníbal González has noted, "The attention paid to Modernism by contemporary Spanish American narrators [e.g., Carpentier and García Márquez] strongly suggests that its legacy is by no means limited to poetry, and that Modernism was, to borrow a phrase from Paz, 'a literature of foundation.'"[13] The journalistic "laboratory" Darío referred to was a generational one. Because publishing outlets were so limited, journalistic venues constituted the main arena for publication. With mass education movements already established in many parts of the Americas, readership grew dramatically just as printing technologies speeded production and distribution. In a way, the publishing circuits were like the railroad networks created in the second half of the nineteenth century, establishing new circuits for both physical and commercial transport as well as intellectual exchange.[14] The *crónica* (chronicle), short journalistic commentaries that transmitted vividly the sights and activities of the cities, became a favorite vehicle for modernista expression, often featuring a distinctively personal voice.[15] Cuban José Martí's *crónicas*, especially those written in New York, and those of Mexican Gutiérrez Nájera ("El Duque Job") serve as windows to understanding urban space in the Americas in their encounters with modernity's upheavals. In the hands of other writers, the *crónica* could become part orientalist travelogue to exotic sites (Guatemala's Gómez Carrillo), cultural commentary (Darío, del Casal), or close to fiction (José Asunción Silva).

We cannot leave the topic of *modernismo* without situating it within the intersection of events that would reorient Latin America's position to both Spain and the United States. The Spanish American War of 1898, in which Spain lost its last remaining colonies (Cuba, Puerto Rico, the Philippines, Guam) to the United States, had a profound effect not only on economic and political alignments, but on intellectual alliances as well. José Enrique Rodó's *Ariel* (1900), the Uruguayan essayist's call to Latin America's youth to rediscover their roots in classical civilization and to reject the materialism that he characterized as an essential part of Anglo-American cultures, had a profound effect on intellectuals. The ripple effect of *arielismo* went far beyond its creator's aims, inspiring both an interest in humanism in opposition to science and technology as well as an aversion to the United States, then entering its period of world power.

The Spanish American War and *arielismo* are not only turning points for international relations and intellectual routes. The dynamic they set in motion helps us to understand the complex undercurrents of the fiction of the period. Writers like Lugones and his colleague Ingenieros were fascinated by science, its marvels and mysteries, including the occult sciences.[16] Darwinism, the science of genetics, and the writings of positivists like Herbert Spencer (who appears regularly in periodicals of the period and was a major influence on Ingenieros) converged to accelerate sweeping programs of national reform that sought to jumpstart the progress of Latin American societies. In other parts of the Western world governments took on the task of institutionalizing public health, sexuality, criminality, transportation, and education. New prosperity in parts of Latin America accelerated these same processes. In particular, the governments of Argentina, Uruguay, Brazil, and Mexico adapted social reforms designed to "improve" and manage their populations.[17] "Progress" itself was highly inflected by notions of scientific racism,[18] theories that complicated and shadowed Rodó's drive to return to "classical" roots. It is worth remembering that Sarmiento's earlier prescription for Argentina, the promotion of European immigration to populate the country and improve its native stock, had unforeseen consequences as racial categories became redefined to disadvantage immigrants from southern Europe. José Ramón Ramos Mejía, doctor and sociologist, in 1899 published the influential *Argentine Multitudes*, which outlined states of successive racial development in Argentina. One of the stages was a monstrous hybrid, "half-person, half-animal," and the immigrant stage late in the century was in a state of metamorphosis like an embryo.[19] The organic metaphors so prevalent in scientific, social, and political discourses undergo often bizarre transformations when interpreted in fiction and poetry.

One of the richest sources of fictional innovation in the period arises from science and government-sponsored programs of progress and reform as they intersect or clash with the individual subject. What happens when societies attempt to organize themselves from the top down, classifying and reorganizing units of society according to the most productive plan? As stories like "Yzur" in this volume make achingly clear, Lugones's creative works often moved against the grain of his political pronouncements. As an artist, he entered into the murky waters of the individual's uneasy response to genetic experimentation, the classification of madness, the criminalization of sexualities, the potentially life-numbing effects of education, and the apocalyptic scenarios of transgression. Josefina Ludmer, who has explored the fascination and danger of Lugones's generation with transgression and crime, has noted the "anti-state gesture of Lugones's new scientists," their marginal or even outlaw status with respect to officialdom.[20] In fiction, the figure of the monster, so prevalent in the nineteenth century from Frankenstein and the Gothic novel to its transformation in decandentism's sexual fantasies toward the end of the century, spills over into the areas of science and progress. What lies out of bounds—boundaries established by science or doctrines of progress—must be categorized as criminal, deviant, or simply unhealthy.[21]

The stories in this volume are not simply cautionary tales or pronouncements on society. Two of his major volumes of short stories, *Strange Forces* (1906) and *Fatal Tales* (1924), are linked to the fantastic, mixing elements of science, the occult, and the Bible and ancient myth. The stories of *The Gaucho*

War (1905) are united in their topic of the wars of independence in 1817 in northwestern Argentina. Aside from the plaquette *Stories* (1916), he published only three volumes of short stories, though he published many other stories dispersed in various publications.[22] Like the title *Strange Forces*, characters (including animals) move amidst powers they do not understand or even know exist. In "The Rain of Fire," a man of great wealth, devoted to physical pleasures although somewhat solitary, experiences the terror of rain that burns like molten metal and exterminates his whole city and his cherished way of life. The fire seems to be a punishment, like the biblical destruction of Sodom and Gomorrah noted in the story's epigraph, yet there are no specifics on what crime or sin provoked it. The details of the story—the enjoyment of the riches of daily life with its food and drink contrasted to the scorching smell of burning flesh—draw our attention to the human condition, not to a possible system of values or forces in control. Helpless and doomed, the human subject is reduced to its animal condition, running for shelter from unseen forces. "Yzur," the story of a monkey's speech lessons, shows, through the "sham of scientific inquiry,"[23] the odd encounter of two species, where the monkey, bought by the narrator in the first lines of the story, is on the path to becoming human. The narrator's pedagogical quest, to teach the monkey to speak, leads him to the brink of madness. Intent on his project, he is unrelenting despite the monkey's sickness and death agony, which finally yields, he thinks, the desired humanizing but enslaved result, sealing his mastery of the situation. The scientist narrates the impetus of his quest, "the demon of analysis, which is only the spirit of perversity," as a counterargument of the exploration. One can only speculate on what emphasis Lugones placed on this story, yet surely his years as an inspector of schools provide an uncanny contribution to this strange tale of educational violence.

Like "Yzur," "Viola Acherontia" explores the twisted potential of scientific exploration, here in the context of plant genetics. The curious narrator is fascinated by the experiments of a gardener who wants to produce the "flower of death." In some ways the story evokes Nathaniel Hawthorne's story "Rappaccini's Daughter" (1846), where an ill-fated love story is entwined with an evil botanist's experiments. Lugones's story omits romance but weaves together suggestions from real scientific studies to lead to a chillingly plausible (within the studies' logic) conclusion.

"The Horses of Abdera" continues the fascination with education and with the exchange of animal and human behavior, especially linguistic faculties, at the same time that it plays with theories of government. The horses, here in the role of those governed, can talk, have their own names and cemeteries, have mirrors in their stables, and even come to the dinner table. Raised in freedom, they become increasingly intelligent and show signs of subversion and outright rebellion. They rape and pillage the human community until the appearance of an enormous feline monster frightens them away. The community, more frightened of this monster than of its own "civilized beasts," despairs until the monster reveals himself— as Hercules! As Borges has noted, this deus ex machina solves a bit too neatly the dilemma of transposition of humans and beasts; nonetheless, the story is forceful beyond its function as a parable of government and (excessive) freedoms.

"The Pillar of Salt" clearly refers to the Old Testament story of Lot's wife and repeats the insistence on punishment and apocalypse of "The Rain of Fire." Here, "to

awaken mystery is a criminal madness, perhaps a temptation from hell." The pious monk, tempted by the devil to
absolve Lot's wife from her millennial petrification, like
other hapless characters in these stories, demands that she
speak. He wants to know the unknowable, what she saw
as she looked back while defying God's orders. Wanting
to know too much, he traffics with the devil and takes on
the forbidden power of bringing the dead back to life. The
monk's asceticism ("Only those who must expiate great
crimes undergo such solitudes") plays against the sensuality
of the main character of "The Rain of Fire." For a story so
centered in a hermit's life, it is full of richly detailed, even
distracting, descriptions. Is it a satire of religion? Although
it is perhaps less satisfying than some of the other stories,
the satiric hints relate it less to the world of science or the
occult than to a veiled commentary on writing itself.

"The *Escuerzo*" strikes another tone, this time of folk legends, but animals and humans again share roles. Animals as
insignificant as toads cannot plot vengeance against their
powerful human enemies, yet in this story folk wisdom
knows truths that rational skeptics ignore. Free of the sty-
listic overload of some of Lugones's prose, the tale has a
rural setting that prefigures the importance such scenes will
play in his later poetry and fiction, as in *Poemas solariegos*.

Later in his career Lugones became especially dedicated to the Greek tradition, a quest that led him to seek
and find in Argentina the kind of epic heroes represented
in Greek civilization. Just as nineteenth-century European
scholars "rediscovered" foundational national epics, so
Lugones's exploration and glorification of the gaucho
tradition led him to establish José Hernández's nineteenth-
century epic *Martín Fierro* as a foundational myth for

Argentine civilization. Expanding the perspective on iden-
titarian movements beyond Argentina, Noé Jitrik sums
up the growing traditionalism of Lugones, the writer who
scoured the globe for creative inspiration and daring but
who returned to a hardened and domesticated nationalism.
According to Jitrik, as liberalism entered into crisis through
popular and leftist movements, spurred on by vast nonas-
similated immigration, there arose a widespread reflection
on national identity, parallel to similar reflections in Spain
in the wake of the disaster of 1898: "Hispanism . . . had, once
again, a dual path: one was aristocratic, purist, and chauvin-
ist, the other popular or populist. In Lugones we find both,
although in succession; first, with the rediscovery of the
gaucho tradition, he reclaims a mixed origin, with a remote,
telluric foundation. Later, as he is seduced by the power of
the gun, his rhetoric takes on a defensive tone with respect
to the foreign immigrant 'invasion.'"[24] Almost every student
of Lugones has noticed similar contradictions, whether in
relation to Hispanism, socialism, classicism, fascism, or the
role of the writer itself.

By the time Lugones became a full-fledged writer, the
relatively secure vantage point of the writer had been un-
done by modernity's embrace of multiple subjectivities and
relative knowledge. His strong impulse toward the formation of a unitary consciousness, his continuing faith in the
role of the strong and directing intellect as a force for society,
coexists with the haunting consciousness that knowledge
in itself, and especially its imposition on others, may be a dangerous thing. This coexistence or convergence of opposing
beliefs sets off an uneasiness in his fiction and poetry. We
could perhaps call this a crisis of subjectivity, an unmooring
of certainties that, despite Lugones's acclaimed erudition

and productiveness, generated the tensions that still draw us to his work. The promise of egalitarianism for erasing divisions of class, language, and knowledge also brought with it mystery and danger, just as scientific and educational experimentation could become threatening and lead to degeneration. The conventions of the "fantastic" mode allow him to give fuller rein to insights or doubts that cannot find a place in a more realistic literary universe. Although his language may seem out of step with our times, its generative machines laboring too hard, producing excesses in language that can seem parodic, in many ways it transmits the unease of a world feverishly populated with new and contradictory bits of knowledge. While Lugones as a political writer took hard and clear stands so that we can trace his political evolution in a perfect arc, in his fiction we see him moving back and forth, making and unmaking a world of words that only hint at what he sensed lay outside of the human grasp.

Notes

1. Lugones and Quiroga, considered founders of the modern short story in Latin America, first met in the literary circles of Buenos Aires. When Lugones was commissioned to travel to the north of Argentina to write *The Jesuit Empire* (1909), the Uruguayan Quiroga accompanied him as official photographer. The trip to Misiones led to Quiroga's fascination with the area, where he often returned to escape from modern life. This region provided Quiroga with the material for some of his most memorable stories about the struggle with nature.

2. The journal *Nosotros*, a journal in which Lugones regularly published, dedicated an issue to him shortly after his death. The successive suicides of Horacio Quiroga (1937), Lugones (1938), and Alfonsina Storni (1938), three of the most notable writers of the day in Argentina,

fueled this reflection on the status of writers. It is interesting to compare this issue with a 1974 publication marking the centenary of his birth. The magazine *Crisis* (no. 14 [June 1974]) includes an article and dossier compiled by Jorge Rivera and reflects the tensions of that extraordinary moment in Argentina's history.

3. Interview with Fernando Sorrentino, quoted in Rafael Olea Franco, "Borges y la *Antología de la literatura fantástica,*" *Variaciones Borges* 22 (2006), 271 (my translation).

4. *Artificial Respiration,* tr. Daniel Balderston (Durham, N.C.: Duke University Press, 1994), 117.

5. Throughout his life Lugones continued to occupy a series of municipal and government positions, as inspector of schools and director of libraries. In later life, despite his increasing closeness to the inner circles of government, he did not receive any lucrative appointments.

6. Rubén Darío, "Un poeta socialista," in *Escritos inéditos de Rubén Darío,* ed. E. K. Mapes (New York: Instituto de las Españas, 1938), 102–103.

7. Octavio Paz, *Cuadrivio,* 2d ed. (Mexico: Joaquín Mortiz, 1969), 36 (my translation).

8. See Tulio Halperín Donghi, *Historia contemporánea de América Latina* (Madrid: Alianza, 1970), 280–282. In English, *Contemporary History of Latin America,* tr. John C. Chasteen (Durham, N.C.: Duke University Press, 1993), and David Rock, *Argentina 1516–1987* (Berkeley: University of California Press, 1987).

9. *Las primeras letras de Leopoldo Lugones* (Buenos Aires: Ediciones Centurión, 1963) (my translation). This is a collection of Lugones's assorted periodical writings from 1893 to 1900 with an introduction and notes by his son, Leopoldo Lugones, hijo.

10. *El payador y antología de poesía y prosa,* ed. Guillermo Ara (Caracas: Ayacucho, 1979), 15.

11. See the new edition, *La montaña* (Buenos Aires: Universidad Nacional de Quilmes, 1998).

12. Octavio Electro Corvalán, "La madurez de Leopoldo Lugones" (Ph.D. diss., Yale University, 1971), 4.

13. *Journalism and the Development of Spanish American Narrative* (Cambridge: Cambridge University Press, 1993), 85.

14. For excellent studies of literary journalism in Latin America, see Boyd G. Carter, *Las revistas literarias de Hispanoamérica* (Mexico: Ediciones de Andres, 1959) and Aníbal González, *Journalism and the Development of Spanish American Narrative* (Cambridge: Cambridge University Press, 1993).

15. The tradition has continued in Latin America: three contemporary *cronistas* are Carlos Monsiváis (Mexico), María Moreno (Argentina), and Pedro Lemebel (Chile).

16. See Fabián Banga, "Lugones y el espiritismo," *Lucero* (2005), http://eter.org/eter/articulos/lugones_espiri.html.

17. Nancy Stepan's *The Hour of Eugenics* (Ithaca, N.Y.: Cornell University Press, 1991) gives a fascinating account of the transformative power of eugenics in Latin America.

18. In Argentina, Carlos Octavio Bunge's *Nuestra América* (1903) presented racial theories based on scientific determinism, equating spiritual supremacy with the white races. See also Richard Graham, ed., *The Idea of Race in Latin America, 1870–1940* (Austin: University of Texas Press, 1990).

19. Gabrielle Nouzeilles, "The Transcultural Mirror of Science: Race and Self-Representation in Latin America" in *Latin American Literary History*, vol. 3, ed. Mario J. Valdés and Djelal Kakir (Oxford: Oxford University Press, 2004), 293.

20. *The Corpus Delicti: A Manual of Argentine Fictions,* tr. Glen S. Close (Pittsburgh: University of Pittsburgh Press, 2004), 66.

21. For further studies on medicine, criminality, and sexuality during this epoch in Argentina, see Jorge Salessi, *Médicos, maricas, y maleantes: Higiene, criminología y homosexualidad en la construcción de la nación Argentina (Buenos Aires: 1871–1914)* (Rosario: B. Viterbo Editora, 1995); Gabriela Nouzeilles, *Ficciones somáticas: Naturalismo, nacionalismo y políticas médicas del cuerpo (Argentina 1880–1910)* (Buenos Aires: Beatriz Viterbo, 2000) and her "The Transcultural Mirror of Science: Race and Self-Representation in Latin America" in *Latin American Literary History*, vol. 3, ed. Mario J. Valdés and Djelal Kadir (Oxford: Oxford University Press, 2004), 284–299; and Diego Armus, ed., *Disease in the History of Modern Latin America, from Malaria to AIDS* (Durham, N.C.: Duke University Press, 2003).

22. Pedro Luis Barcia edited and annotated a collection of these dispersed stories in *Leopoldo Lugones: Cuentos desconocidos* (Buenos Aires: Ediciones del 80, 1982).

23. Howard M. Fraser, "Modernism's Dismantling of Scientific Discourse," *Hispania* 79, no. 1 (Mar. 1996), 8–19. This story has evoked a number of intriguing readings. Jorge Schwartz's "De simios y antropófagas. Los monos de Lugones, Vallejo y Kafka" is a creative reading of the man/monkey question (*Nuevo Texto Crítico,* año XII, no.23/24 [1999], 155–168). Adriana Rodríguez Pérsico, in "Sueños modernos, viejas pesadillas. Usos literarios de hipótesis científicas," compares Quiroga's story "The Hanged Monkey" with "Yzur" in exploring relations of dominance and linguistic power (http://www.iafe.uba.ar/relatividad/gangui/ sigmaxi/mesa/files_mesajunio/mesa_ach_arpersico). Julio Ramos reads "Yzur" in terms of the representation of the national subaltern, both linguistically and ethnically, in "Faceless Tongues: Language and Citizenship in Nineteenth-Century Latin America," in *Displacements: Cultural Identities in Question*, ed. Angelika Bammer (Bloomington: Indiana University Press, 1994), 25–46.

24. *Leopoldo Lugones: Mito nacional* (Buenos Aires: Ediciones Palestra, 1960), 128–129 (my translation).

Fiction:
Short Stories

The Rain of Fire

from *Strange Forces* (1906)

Evocation of a Disembodied Soul from Gomorrah[1]

> And I will make your heaven as iron, and your earth as brass.
> —*Leviticus 26:19*[2]

I remember that it was a beautiful, sunny day, the streets swarming with people and deafening vehicles. An abundantly warm day, with a perfect feel about it.

From my terrace I stood above a vast confusion of rooftops, the occasional garden, a strip of bay punctuated by masts, the gray stretch of an avenue ...

The first sparks fell around eleven o'clock. One here, another there—particles of copper like those of a candlewick;

particles of iridescent copper hitting the ground with the slight sound of something dropping in sand. The sky remained as clear as before, and the urban din did not decrease. Only the birds in my birdcages ceased their singing.

I noticed it by chance, looking out toward the horizon in a moment of abstraction. At first I thought it an optical illusion brought about by my myopia. I had to wait a long while to see another spark fall, for the rays from the sun negated them considerably; but the copper burned in such a way that they were still detectable. A quick dash of fire, and the little strike on the ground. And so it went, separated by long intervals.

I must confess that when I confirmed that it was true, I experienced a vague terror. I examined the sky with an anxious gaze. The clearness persisted. From where did that strange hail come? That copper? Was it copper? . . .

A spark had just fallen on my terrace, a few steps away. I stretched my hand out; it was, without a doubt, a grain of copper that took a long time to cool. Luckily the breeze was picking up, shifting the extraordinary rain toward the opposite end of my terrace. In addition, the sparks were quite sparse. One could believe for a moment that it had ceased. But it had not ceased. One here, another there, that is true, yet the frightful granules continued to fall.

Still, this rain would not impede me from lunching, for it was midday. I went down through the garden to the dining room, not without a certain fear of the sparks. It is true that the canopy, drawn to block the sun, protected me . . .

Did it protect me? I looked up; but the canopy had so many overlapping seams that I could not determine anything.

An admirable lunch awaited me in the dining room; in my happy celibacy I knew two things above all: reading and eating. After my library, the dining room was my pride. Fed up with women and a bit gouty, I could no longer expect anything other than gluttony from the amiable vices. I ate alone, while a slave read me geographic narratives. I have never been able to understand eating with company; and if women annoy me, as I have said, you will of course understand that I abhor men.

Ten years separated me from my last orgy! Since then, devoted to my gardens, to my fish, to my birds, I had not enough time to go out. Sometimes, in the very hot afternoons, a stroll to the edge of the lake. I enjoyed looking at the waters of the lake, scalloped by the moon at nightfall, but that was all, and I would go months without going there.

The vast libertine city was for me a desert where my pleasures took refuge. Scarce friends, brief visits, long hours at the table, readings, my fish, my birds, occasionally an evening with an orchestra of flautists, and two or three attacks of gout per year . . .

I had the honor of being consulted for city banquets, and in these they had included, with some praise, two or three recipes of my invention. This gave me the right—I say it without pride—to a municipal statue, as justified as that of the lady compatriot who recently invented the latest kiss.

Meanwhile, my slave read. He read narratives of the sea and of the snow, and these added, now that we were well into the siesta, a wonderful commentary to the generous freshness of the amphoras.[3] The rain of fire had perhaps ceased, for the servants gave no sign of having noticed it.

Suddenly, the slave crossing the garden with a new dish was unable to hold back a scream. Although he was able to reach the table, his pallor revealed a horrible pain. On his naked back he had a small hole, at the bottom of which could still be heard the sizzling of the voracious spark that had opened it. We drowned it out with oil, and he was sent to his bed, unable to contain his laments.

Abruptly I lost my appetite; and although I continued tasting the dishes so as to not demoralize the servants, they very quickly understood. The incident had left me disconcerted.

Halfway through the siesta I climbed once again up to the terrace. The ground was already sowed with grains of copper; but it did not appear that the rain was increasing. I was starting to grow more peaceful, when a new restlessness came over me. The silence was absolute. The traffic was paralyzed, doubtlessly because of the phenomenon. Not a single sound in the city. Only, every once in a while, a vague rustling of the wind through the trees. Also alarming was the attitude of the birds. They had piled up in a corner almost on top of one another. I felt compassion for them and decided to open their doors. They did not want to go out; rather, they withdrew further, even more distressed. At that point I began to feel daunted at the thought of a cataclysm.

Although my scientific erudition was not great, I knew that no one had ever mentioned such rains of incandescent copper. Rains of copper! There are no copper mines in the air. Then there was that clearness of the skies, so that one could not conjecture as to the source of the rain. And this was the alarming aspect of the phenomenon. The sparks came from everywhere and from nowhere at once. It was immensity itself being torn invisibly into fire. The terrible copper was falling from the firmament—but the firmament remained impassibly blue. A strange distress began slowly to come over me; but there was something strange: until then I had not thought about escaping. Escaping! And my table, my books, my birds, my fish that had just recently moved into a new pond, my gardens already ennobled in their years, my fifty years of serenity, in the good fortune of today, in the carelessness of tomorrow . . . ?

Escaping! And I thought in horror of my properties (which I had never seen) on the other side of the desert—where the cameleers live in tents of black wool and take, as their only nourishment, curdled milk, toasted wheat, sour honey . . .

There was still an escape route remaining, by crossing the lake, but this would be a brief escape at best, if it was also raining copper on the lake, as it was in the desert. And it was certainly logical to assume as much, for as it did not come from any visible focal point, the fiery rain must be everywhere.

Notwithstanding the vague, alarming terror, I was able to say all these things to myself clearly, debating within myself, a bit debilitated, if truth be told, by the digestive lethargy of my customary siesta. And, after all, something told me that the phenomenon would not go any further. Still, nothing was lost by having my car loaded.

At that moment the air was filled with a vast vibration of bells tolling. And almost at once, I noticed something: it was no longer raining copper. The tolling was a gesture of gratefulness, accompanied almost immediately by the usual sounds of the city, awaking from its brief atony, twice as noisy as usual. In some neighborhoods petards were even being lighted.

Leaning on the parapet of the terrace, I looked on with an unknown, solitary well-being at the vespertine bustling commotion that was all love and lust. The skies were still of the purest blue. Eager young men gathered the metal shavings of copper in small shields, and copper makers had already begun to buy them. That was all that was left of the great light-blue threat.

More numerous than ever, people of pleasure colored the streets; and I still recall that I smiled vaguely at an equivocal adolescent, whose tunic, gathered up to his hips as he jumped at a street intersection, revealed his smooth legs, checkered with ribbons. The courtesans, their breasts naked and propped up by brilliant corsets according to the latest fashion, walked about indolently, perspiring perfumes. An old procurer drove by upright in his car, as if he were a lighted torch, holding up a tin sheet displaying, in proportioned paintings, the monstrous loves of beasts: couplings of lizards with swans; a monkey and a seal; a maiden draped like a peacock in delirious jewels. A beautiful display, upon my word; and the authenticity of the pieces guaranteed. Animals tamed by some unknown barbaric spell, and unbalanced with opium and asafetida.[4]

A very friendly Negro passed by, followed by three masked youths; the Negro drew intimate scenes with lavish colors on patios while dancing in rhythm. He also depilated with yellow orpiment[5] and knew how to gild fingernails.

A flimsy character, whose condition as an eunuch could be guessed by his suppleness, was peddling—to the sound of bronze finger cymbals—bedspreads made of a unique weaving that produced insomnia and desire. Bedspreads that upright citizens had requested be abolished. Thus my city knew how to take pleasure, how to live.

When night fell I received two visitors to dine with me. A jovial colleague—a mathematician whose unruly life was the scandal of science—and an agriculturist who had grown wealthy. People felt the need to visit each other after the rain of copper sparks. To visit and to drink, for both men left completely inebriated. I made a quick exit. The city, capriciously illuminated, had taken advantage of the occasion to decree a night of celebration. In the cornices of some buildings, lamps of incense perfumed as well as illuminated. From their balconies, young bourgeois ladies, excessively adorned, entertained themselves by blowing painted streamers and crackling rattles down on distracted passersby. There was dancing on every corner. Flowers and small candies were exchanged from one balcony to another. The park lawns throbbed with couples . . .

I came back early, worn out. Never had I taken refuge in bed more grateful to feel the heaviness of sleep.

I woke up soaked in perspiration, my eyes clouded over, my throat dry. There was a murmuring of rain outside. Searching for something, I leaned against the wall, and a tremor of fear snapped like a whip through my body. The wall was hot and vibrating silently. It was almost unnecessary for me to open the window to realize what was happening.

The rain of fiery copper had returned, but this time dense and constant. A murky fume suffocated the city; a smell part phosphorous and part urinous infected the air. Luckily, my house was surrounded by galleries and the rain could not reach its doors.

I opened the door leading out to the garden. The trees were black, already bared of their foliage; the ground, covered with charred leaves. The air, torn by dashes of fire, was deadly paralyzed; and between the fiery shreds could be seen the firmament, always impassible, always sky blue.

I called out, I called out in vain. I checked everywhere, even the domestic chambers. The servants had all left. I was able to reach the stables by wrapping my legs in a byssus[6] covering and armoring my back and head with a metal tub that was crushing me tremendously. The horses had disappeared as well. And with a peacefulness that served my nerves well, I realized I was lost.

Luckily, the dining room was full of provisions, and my cellar abounded with wines. It still preserved its coolness; neither the vibrations of the heavy rain, nor the echo of its grave crackling, reached the depths of the cellar. I drank a bottle, and then removed the flask of poisoned wine from a secret cupboard. Everyone who had a bodega had one, although it was not used even when one had burdensome guests. It was a clear, flavorless liqueur, with instantaneous effects.

Revived by the wine, I considered my situation. It was rather simple. Unable to escape, death awaited me; but with this poison, I owned death. So I decided to observe the event as much as possible, for it was, without a doubt, a unique spectacle. A rain of incandescent copper! The city in flames! This was certainly worth watching.

I went up to the terrace, but was unable to pass through the access door. I could see enough from there, however. I could see and listen. The solitude was absolute. The crackling was uninterrupted except for the occasional howling of a dog, or by some abnormal explosion. The air was red; and through it, trunks, chimneys, and houses turned whitish with an exceedingly sad wanness. The few trees that still maintained any foliage writhed, black as blackened tin. The light had dimmed somewhat, notwithstanding the persistence of the sky-blue clearness. The horizon was much closer, however, as if drowning in ashes. A thick vapor floated above the lake, partially compensating for the extraordinary dryness of the air.

The combustible rain could be seen clearly: strips of copper that vibrated like the innumerable strings of a harp, occasionally trailing flaming pennants. Black billows of smoke indicated fires here and there.

My birds were starting to die of thirst, so I went down to the cistern to retrieve water for them. The cellar was connected to this water well, a vast deposit that could resist the celestial fire for a long time; but a certain amount of copper had slid down from the channels flowing from the rooftops and the patios, giving the water a peculiar salty taste, like a mix between natron[7] and urine. However, all I had to do was raise the mosaic slats to disconnect the channels and close off my water from all contact with the outside.

That afternoon and the entire night the spectacle of the city was horrendous. Burning in their homes, people fled terrified, only to blaze in the streets, in the desolate countryside; and the populace agonized savagely, with laments and wailings of stupendous amplitude, horror, variety. There is nothing as sublime as the human voice. The collapse of the buildings, the combustion of so much merchandise and diverse goods, and more than anything the burning of so many bodies, finally added the torment of their infernal stench to the cataclysm. When the sun went down, the air was nearly black with smoke and clouds of dust. The flaming pennants that danced in the morning among the raining copper were now sinister blazes. An extremely hot, thick wind began to blow, like melted tar. It was as if one were inside an immense, somber oven. Sky, earth, air, everything was ending. There was nothing other than darkness and fire. Oh, the horror of that darkness, which even the fire, the enormous fire of the burning city, could not overcome; and that stench of tatters, of sulfur, of cadaverous fat in the dry air that made one spit blood; and that wailing that somehow did not end, that wailing louder than the crackling of the fire, vaster than a hurricane, that wailing that contained—in its howling, moaning, bellowing—the ineffable, eternal terror of all creatures! . . .

I went down to the cistern; although bristling from head to foot with all that horror, I had not yet lost my spirits. But when I found myself all of a sudden in that friendly darkness, within the refuge of the coolness, before the silence of the subterranean water, I was suddenly overcome by a fear that I had not felt—I am certain—since forty years earlier: the childish fear of an obscure enemy presence. And I began to cry, to cry like a madman, to cry from fear in a corner, without any shame.

It was not until very late, when, upon hearing the collapse of a roof, that it occurred to me to brace the door of the cellar. This I did with its own ladder and some beams from the shelves, a defense that gave me back some degree of tranquility, not because I was to be saved, but because I had at least taken some action. The hours passed as I drowsed off and fell into intermittent fatal nightmares. Constantly I heard things collapsing nearby. I had lighted two lamps that I had brought with me, to give me courage, for the cistern was thoroughly gloomy. I even ate, albeit without appetite, the remainder of a cake. But I did drink a great deal of water.

All of a sudden my lamps began to dim, and with that I was overcome with terror, a paralyzing terror this time. I had used, without realizing it, all of my light, for I had only those two lamps. I had not thought, when I came down that afternoon, to bring all the lamps from the house down with me.

The lights diminished and went out. Then I realized that the cistern was beginning to fill with the stench of the fire. There was nothing left to do but go out; for anything, anything was better than dying asphyxiated like an animal in its cave.

With great effort I was able to raise the cellar top door, covered by the rubble of the dining room . . .

For a second time the infernal rain had ceased. But the city no longer existed. Roofs, doors, a great number of walls, all the towers, lay in ruins. The silence was colossal, without a doubt the silence of catastrophe. Five or six large clouds of smoke still towered high in the air; and under the sky—a sky that had remained undisturbed the entire time, a sky whose coarse blue attested to an eternal indifference—the poor city, my poor city lay dead like a cadaver, dead forever.

The uniqueness of the situation, the enormity of the phenomenon, and also without a doubt the joy of having survived, alone among all, curbed my pain and replaced it with a somber curiosity. The archway of my portico had remained standing, and making use of its toothing, I was able to climb to its apex.

Nothing combustible was left; what had once been my city looked much like a volcanic heap of slag. At intervals, in the places not covered by the ash, the metal that had rained down shone a fiery red. Toward the edge by the desert, a sandy mound of copper gleamed as far as the eye could see. In the mountains, on the other side of the lake, the waters that had evaporated from the latter condensed into a storm. Those were the waters that had kept the air breathable during the cataclysm. The sun shone immensely, and I was beginning to be overwhelmed with a deep desolation of solitude, when I saw a shape wandering among the ruins near the port. It was a man, and he had certainly seen me, for he was heading in my direction.

When he arrived, we did not act as if it was at all unusual that he climbed up the archway and came to sit with me. He turned out to be a pilot who had survived in a cellar, like me, but in his case by stabbing the owner of the cellar to death. He had just run out of water, which is why he had come out.

Having learned this, I began to question him. All the boats, piers, and deposits had burned; the lake had become bitter. Although I realized that we were speaking in low voices, I do not know why but I did not dare to raise mine.

I offered him my bodega, where there were still two dozen hams, some cheeses, all the wine . . .

All of a sudden we noticed a cloud of dust rising from the desert. A dust cloud from racing creatures. Some aid party that had been sent, perhaps, by our compatriots from Admah or from Zeboim.[8]

Soon, though, this hope was replaced with a spectacle as distressing as it was dangerous.

It was a pack of lions, a group of surviving beasts from the desert, turning to the city as an oasis, raving with thirst, driven insane by the cataclysm.

It was thirst and not hunger that maddened them, for they passed us by without notice. And what a state they were in. There was nothing as lugubrious as this sight to reveal the extent of the catastrophe.

Hairless like mangy cats; their manes reduced to scant crisp rinds; their flanks dried-out and, as if half-dressed, in comical disproportion to their large wild heads; their tails bare and charred like those of fleeing rats—all this clearly conveyed their three days of horror under the sky-blue whipping, at the mercy of unsafe caverns in which they had been unable to fully take refuge.

They circled around the dry fountains with a human madness in their eyes, and then abruptly set about their race again in search of another deposit of water, which would be exhausted as well. Finally, they sat around the last one, their scorched jaws in the air, with an eternal, nebulous gaze of desolation—complaining, I am certain—to the heavens, and began to roar.

Oh . . . nothing, not even the cataclysm with its horrors, nor the wailing of the moribund city, was as horrendous as the cry of those wild beasts sitting among the ruins. Those roars communicated as intelligibly as words. Who knows what unconscious anguish of abandonment they cried to what dark divinity. The succinct soul of the beast added the terror of the incomprehensible to its fear of dying. If everything was the same—the quotidian sun, the eternal sky, the familiar desert—why were they burning and why was there no water . . . ? And lacking the possibility of forming any thought about the relationship between phenomena, their horror was blind—even more dreadful, that is. Their transporting anguish elevated them, before those skies from where that infernal rain had fallen, toward some notion of originating source; and their roaring clearly demanded some explanation of the tremendous event that had caused their suffering. Oh . . . that roaring, the only grandeur left of those diminished wild animals: how it glossed the horrendous secret of the catastrophe; how it spoke, in its irremediable pain, of eternal solitude, of eternal silence, of eternal thirst . . .

But it was not to last for long. It began to rain candescent metal anew, denser and heavier than ever.

In our rushed descent, we managed to see that the beasts scattered, searching for shelter under the rubble.

We reached the cellar, not without being hit by a few sparks; and understanding that this new shower would consummate the ruin, I prepared myself for the end.

While my companion took advantage of the bodega—for the first and the last time, without a doubt—I decided to make use of the water from the cistern for my funereal bath; and after searching in vain for a piece of soap, I entered the cistern by walking down the steps used for its cleaning.

I carried with me the flask of poison; this gave me a great well-being, which was barely disturbed by the curiosity of death.

The cool water and the darkness gave me back the voluptuousness of my existence as a wealthy man, which I had just decided to end. Submerged up to my neck, the joy of being clean and a sweet sense of domesticity completed the calming effect.

Outside I could hear the hurricane of fire. The rubble was starting to fall again. Not a single sound could be heard from the bodega. I noticed at that point the reflection of flames making their way through the cellar door, the characteristic urinous fumes . . . I brought the flask to my lips, and . . .

Yzur

from *Strange Forces* (1906)

I purchased the monkey at the auction of a circus that had closed down.

One afternoon, I was reading somewhere that the natives of Java attribute the lack of an articulated language in monkeys not to their inability to practice it, but to their abstention from it—and that was the first time it occurred to me to attempt the experiment to which these lines are dedicated. "They do not speak," the article reported the natives saying, "so that they will not be forced to work."

Such an idea, not so profound at first, eventually preoccupied me and grew into the following anthropological postulate:

I maintain that monkeys were once men who, for some reason or another, have stopped talking. This silence subsequently produced an atrophy of their phonic organs and of the language centers in their brains; it weakened, almost to the point of suppression, the relationship between these organs and centers, reducing the language of the species to inarticulate screams, leading to the degeneration of these primitive humans into their current animality.

It was clear that if I were able to demonstrate this, I could explain all the anomalies that make the monkey such a unique being; and there was only one possible way to prove this: to return the monkey to language.

In the meantime, I traveled all around with mine, the whole time further connecting him to the world through adventures and unexpected events. In Europe he attracted a great deal of attention, and if I had wished it, I could have bestowed upon him the celebrity of a consul; but my seriousness as a businessman did not agree with such clowning around.

Driven by my firm idea about the language of monkeys, I exhausted all the bibliography relating to the issue, without any appreciable results. I knew only, with entire certainty, *that there was no scientific reason for monkeys not to speak.* This after five years of pondering the subject.

Yzur (I was never able to discover the origin of this name, as his previous owner did not know it either) was certainly a noteworthy animal. His circus education, albeit reduced almost entirely to mimicry, had helped him develop his faculties quite a bit; and this encouraged me even further to pursue my seemingly absurd theory upon him.

Still, it is known that the chimpanzee (which Yzur was) is, of all the monkeys, the best endowed with brains and one of the most docile, increasing my probabilities of success. My conviction of his stunted humanity was increased every time that I saw him walking upright, his hands behind his back to keep balance, looking very much like a drunken sailor.

There is really no good reason why monkeys cannot articulate completely. Their natural language, which is to say the set of screams with which they communicate among themselves, is quite varied; their larynx, as different as it may be from that of humans, is not nearly as different as that of the parrot, which nonetheless speaks; and with regards to their brains, besides the fact that comparisons with birds should dismiss any doubt, suffice it to recall that the brain of a half-wit is also rudimentary, despite which there are some cretins who are able to utter a number of words. And in regards to Broca's convolution,[1] it depends, of course, on the total development of the brain; besides that it is not *altogether* proven that this area is the site of the localization of language. Even though it may be the best-established anatomical site of localization, there are clearly irrefutable cases that contradict this hypothesis.[2]

Luckily monkeys have, among their many bad qualities, a taste for learning, as demonstrated by their imitative tendencies; a fortunate memory; the power of reflection, which even allows them a sophisticated ability to deceive; and an attention span comparatively more developed than that of a child. They are, in effect, one of the most favorable of pedagogical subjects.

Mine was also young, and it is known that youth constitutes the monkey's best intellectual period and that it is similar in this to the Negro. The difficulty resided solely in the method that I would use to communicate to him the faculty of speech.

I knew the fruitless attempts of all of my predecessors, and it may be unnecessary to say so, but facing competition from several of them, and knowing the uselessness of all their efforts, my own designs failed more than once; it was then, however, that thinking so thoroughly about this topic brought me to the following conclusion:

The first step consists in developing the monkey's apparatus for vocalization.

This is, in effect, how one proceeds with deaf-mutes, before getting them to articulate words; and no sooner had I thought of this, than the analogies between deaf-mutes and monkeys rushed to my mind.

First of all, extraordinary mimetic motion, when used to compensate for articulated speech, proves that one does not necessarily cease to think when one ceases to speak, even if the former faculty is diminished by the latter's paralysis. Then, there are other, more peculiar, because more specific, characteristics: a diligence in work, fidelity, and courage, increased in all certainty by these two conditions, truly revelatory in their connection; an ease in exercises of equilibrium; and a resistance to dizziness.

I thus decided to begin my work by submitting my monkey's lips and tongue to a veritable gymnastics, treating him in this as if he were a deaf-mute. For the rest of it, I favored the ear to establish direct connections with words, without the need to rely on the faculty of touch. The reader will see that in this I prejudged with too much optimism.

Luckily, the chimpanzee is, of all the great apes, the one with the most mobile of lips; and in his particular case, because Yzur had suffered from angina, he already knew how to open his mouth for an examination.

My first inspection partially confirmed my suspicions. His tongue remained at the bottom of his mouth, like an inert mass, moving only when he had to swallow. The gymnastics produced the desired effect, for in two months he already knew how to jest by sticking his tongue out. This was the first relationship that he learned between the movement of his tongue and a specific idea; a relationship that was, in addition, perfectly in accordance with his nature.

The lips were more work, and I was even forced to stretch them out for him with forceps; but he appreciated—perhaps from my reactions—the importance of this anomalous task, and he undertook it keenly. While I practiced the labial movements that he was to imitate, he remained sitting, scratching his rump with his arm stretched back, frowning in dubious concentration, or caressing his side-whiskers with all the attitude of a man who organizes his thoughts through such rhythmic gestures. Finally, he learned to move his lips.

But the exercise of language is a difficult art, as proven by a child's long periods of babbling, which eventually lead him, in parallel to his intellectual development, to the acquisition of the habits necessary for speech. It is demonstrated, in effect, that the very center of the innervations of vowels is associated to such an extent with that of the word in which the vowels appear, that the normal development of both depends upon their harmonized practice. Heinicke—the inventor of the oral method for teaching deaf-mutes—had already predicted this connection, as a philosophical consequence, in 1785.[3] He spoke of a "dynamic concatenation of ideas," a phrase whose deep clarity more than one psychologist working today would be honored to have uttered.

Yzur found himself, with respect to language, in the same situation as a child who already understands many words before being able to speak them; however, because he had had more experiences in life, he was much more apt at establishing the kinds of judgments that he should hold over different things.

His judgment was sound not only when he encountered something for the first time, it was also of an inquisitive and disquisitive nature—this being based on the differential character that his decisions assumed, and on the fact that such an approach presupposes the power of abstract reasoning. All this lent him a superior level of intelligence, which was certainly quite favorable for my goals.

If my theories seem too bold, consider then that syllogisms—in other words, fundamentally logical arguments—are not foreign to the minds of many animals, as syllogisms are originally a comparison between two sensations. If not, why do animals that know man flee from him, while those that have never known him do not . . .?

I began, then, with Yzur's phonetic education.

My approach was to teach him a word mechanically first, and then to lead him progressively toward that word's meaning.

As the monkey already possessed a voice—in other words, having this advantage, however rudimentary his articulations, over the deaf-mute—my approach was to teach him to modify his existing voice, so as to form the various phonemes and their pronunciation (which are known, according to professors, as either static or dynamic, depending on whether one refers to the articulation of vowels or of consonants).

Given the monkey's gluttony, and following here a method utilized by Heinicke with deaf-mutes, I decided to associate each vowel with a treat: *a* with candy; *e* with sweet; *i* with wine; *o* with cocoa; *u* with sugar, so that the vowel was contained in the sound of the name of the treat, whether it be as the sole, repeated sound of the vowel (as in *cocoa*), or combining the two sounds, with different tonic and prosodic stresses, to form a single utterance: *sugar, candy.*[4]

Everything went well as long as we were working on the vowels, which is to say the sounds formed with an open mouth. Yzur learned them in fifteen days. The *u* was the most difficult one for him to pronounce.[5]

The consonants, on the other hand, gave me a devil of a time; before long I realized that he would never be able to pronounce those that are formed with the use of the teeth and gums. His long canines hindered him altogether.

His vocabulary was reduced, then, to the five vowels and to the *b*, the *k*, the *m*, the *g*, the *f*, and the *c*, which is to say those consonants articulated only with the use of the roof of the mouth and the tongue.

But even for this the ear was insufficient. I had to resort to using the faculty of touch, placing his hand on my chest and then on his, as if he were a deaf-mute, so that he could feel the vibrations of the corresponding sounds.

Three years went by, without my getting him to utter a single word. He tended to name things with the letter whose sound predominated in them, as if that were their proper name. And that was all.

In the circus he had learned to bark, like the dogs that accompanied him in his tasks. And when he saw me become desperate at the vain attempts to tear a word out of him, he would bark loudly, as if he were giving me everything he had. He could articulate vowels and consonants separately but was unable to connect them. At most, he would hit upon a vertiginous repetition of *p*'s and *m*'s.

However, slowly, a great change began to come over his character. There seemed to be less mobility in his facial gestures, and he started to develop a deeper gaze and to assume meditative poses. He acquired, for example, the habit of contemplating the stars. His sensibility was developing at an equal pace; I noted in him a great facility to cry.

The lessons continued with indomitable tenacity, albeit without much success. All this had become a painful obsession for me, and I felt more and more inclined to utilize force. My character was becoming embittered with failure, and I was beginning to assume a silent animosity toward Yzur. Underneath his rebellious muteness, the monkey was becoming more intellectualized, and I was starting to be convinced that I would never shake him from where he was at; it was then that I suddenly realized that, if he was not speaking, it must be by choice.

One night, the cook came to tell me, horrified, that he had caught the monkey saying "actual words." He was, according to the cook's story, hunched down in the orchard by a fig tree; but fright prevented the cook from remembering the crucial part of the story: the words themselves. He thought he could remember only two of them: *bed* and *pipe*. I nearly kicked the imbecile out.

Needless to say, I spent the entire night overcome by a great emotion; and what I had held back from doing for the previous three years, the mistake which would throw everything away, arose as much from the state of my nerves after staying up all night, as from my excessive curiosity.

Instead of allowing the monkey to reach the stage of being able to express himself with language naturally, I called him the next day and tried to impose it upon him through obedience.

I did not get anything out of him other than the *p*'s and *m*'s with which I was so fed up, the hypocritical frowns, and—God forgive me—a certain glimmer of irony in the troubled ubiquity of his grimaces.

I became infuriated and beat him without any restraint. The only thing I achieved with this was to make him shed tears in absolute silence, to the exclusion even of any moaning sounds.

Three days later he fell ill, in a kind of somber dementia complicated by symptoms of meningitis. Leeches, cold affusions, purgatives, cutaneous revulsives, bryony and alcohol solutions: every therapy against the terrible illness was applied. I fought with desperate vigor, driven by remorse and fear. The former because I believed the animal to have fallen victim to my cruelty; the latter from thinking of the fate of the secret that he would perhaps take with him to the grave.

He improved after a long time but remained so weak that he could not get out of bed. The proximity to death had ennobled and humanized him. He did not take his grateful eyes off of me; they followed me around the room like revolving balls, even when I went behind him; and his hands searched for mine with the intimacy of convalescence. In my great solitude, he was very quickly acquiring the importance of a person.

Still, the analytical demon, which is nothing other than a kind of perverting spirit, drove me to renew my experiments. In reality the monkey had spoken. This could not end like this.

I began, very slowly, asking him to say the letters that he knew how to pronounce. Nothing! I left him alone for a few hours, spying through a small hole in the partition wall. Nothing! I spoke to him in brief sentences, trying to appeal to his sense of loyalty or to his gluttony. Nothing! When my sentences were moving ones, his eyes became filled with tears. When I said a common phrase, such as "I am your master," with which I began all my lessons, or "you are my monkey," with which I concluded the previous statement—so as to infuse his spirit with the certainty of an absolute truth—he would assent by closing his eyelids. But he did not utter a single sound or even move his lips.

He had returned to gesticulating as his only form of communicating with me. This detail, combined with the other analogies with deaf-mutes, only served to reinforce my precautions, for no one ignores the predisposition of the latter toward mental illnesses. At times, though, I wished that he would go insane, to see if the delirium would finally break his silence.

His convalescence remained unchanged. The same thinness, the same sadness. It was evident that his mind ailed and that he was in pain. His entire organism had broken down, set off by an abnormal cerebration, and the end was fast approaching—if not today, then tomorrow.

But despite his tameness, which only increased with the progress of the illness, his silence—that despairing silence provoked by my own exasperation—did not cede. From some dark depth of tradition petrified in the animal, race imposed its millenarian muteness, gathering strength from an atavistic will that must have been located at the very roots of his being. These one-time men from the jungles, whose silence—that is: whose intellectual suicide—was caused by some unknown injustice, continued to protect their secret. And this secret, a decision of silence by now unconscious, which lay hidden along with the mysteries of the forests, in the abysses of prehistory, was as formidable as the immensity of time that has since passed.

Such misfortune, that of the backward anthropoid, in the history of evolution, in which the lead was taken by humans with somberly barbaric despotism. Man had doubtlessly dethroned the great Quadrumana[6] families from their primitive Edens in their dominion of the trees, thinning their ranks, capturing their females to organize slavery beginning in the womb itself; until the quadrumanes, in their defeated impotence, were inspired to undertake an act that also led them, unfortunately for the faculty of speech, to break all advanced connections with the enemy. Thus, their act of mortal dignity: to take sanctuary, as an ultimate measure of salvation, in the darkness of their animality.

What horrors, what extreme cruelties the victors must have committed upon the half-beasts in the course of evolution, for them to have resigned themselves—after having tasted the intellectual pleasure of the paradisiacal fruit described in the Bible—to that abandonment of their species, in which they lowered themselves to the level of their inferiors; to that backwardness that would freeze their intelligence forever in the gestures of an acrobat's automatism; to that great cowardice in life, which would eternally curve their backs into the distinctly bestial shape of those that are dominated, imprinting on them that melancholic bewilderment that remains like a caricature at the center of their being.

It was being so close to success before the depths of such atavistic limbo that had awoken my ill humor. After a million years, the incantation of the spoken word moved the old simian soul again, presenting it with a temptation that would have violated the darkness of its sheltering animal nature; but an ancestral memory, which had been disseminated in the species through some instinctive horror for just as much time, was opposing it, strong as a wall.

Yzur entered his death throes without losing consciousness. A bittersweet end—with eyes closed, weakened breathing, inconsistent pulse, in absolute stillness—interrupted only occasionally, when he would turn his face toward me with an eternally heartrending expression, like that of a sad, old mulatto. And on the last afternoon, on the afternoon of his death, the extraordinary occurred, that extraordinary thing that led me to undertake this narration.

I had dozed off at the headboard of his bed, overcome by the heat and the silence of the encroaching dusk, when I suddenly felt something shaking me by the wrist.

I awoke, startled. The monkey, his eyes very wide open, was now definitely dying, and his expression was so human that it filled me with horror. But his hand, his eyes, drew me toward him with such eloquence that I immediately leaned forward, close to his face. And then, with his last breath—the last breath, with which all my hopes were crowned and in which they at once faded—sprung forth—I am certain—sprung forth in a murmur (how to explain a voice that has remained silent for ten thousand centuries?) the following words, the humanity of which reconciled the species:

"Water, master. Master, my master . . ."[7]

Viola Acherontia[1]

from *Strange Forces* (1906)

That strange gardener, what he wanted was to create the flower of death. His attempts dated back ten years, always with negative results; because he believed that plant life had no soul, he paid attention only to their form. Grafts, combinations, he had experimented with everything. The production of a black rose occupied him for a time; but nothing came of his investigations in that area. Then he became interested in passion flowers and tulips, which resulted only in two or three monstrous specimens, until Bernardin de Saint-Pierre[2] put him on the right path, teaching him how one can draw analogies between a flower and a pregnant woman, both supposedly capable of being imprinted with images of desired objects upon a "whim."

Accepting this bold hypothesis was equal to postulating that plants possess an intellect sufficiently elevated to receive, realize, and preserve an impression; in a word, of being suggestible with an intensity similar to that of a superior organism. And this was precisely what our gardener had managed to prove.

He maintained that the tendrils of vines advanced deliberately, obeying a deliberation, followed by a resolution, giving rise to a series of probes. Thus the seemingly capricious layering and curves, the diverse orientations and adaptations on different planes, were executed by the guides, the shoots, the roots. A simple nervous system presided over these dark functions. Each plant also had a cerebral bulb and a rudimentary heart, situated respectively at the neck and the trunk of the roots. The seed, that is, the being reduced for procreation, allowed one to see this with all clarity. The embryo of a nut has the same shape as the heart, while the cotyledon[3] extensively resembles the brain. The two rudimentary leaves that come out of said embryo quite clearly remind one of the two bronchial branches, whose function they carry out upon germination.

Morphological analogies almost always assume other, deeper ones; and thus suggestions can exercise a broader influence over the forms of beings than what is commonly believed. Some clairvoyants from natural history, such as Michelet[4] and Fríes,[5] predicted this truth, which experience has since confirmed. The world of insects proves it entirely. Birds display brighter colors in countries whose skies are always clear (Gould[6]). White cats with blue eyes are usually deaf (Darwin). There are fish that have the waves of the sea photographed on the gelatin of their dorsal fin (Strindberg[7]). The sunflower faces constantly toward the sun and faithfully reproduces its nucleus, rays, and spots (Saint-Pierre[8]).

This was the point of departure. In his *Novum Organum,*[9] Bacon establishes that, when placed close to fetid places, cinnamon and other fragrant plants obstinately retain their aroma, refusing to emit their fragrance to prevent it from mixing with the foul vapors . . .

The extraordinary gardener whom I was going to visit was attempting to instill violets with a new power. He had found them to be uniquely nervous, as demonstrated, he added, by the always exaggerated affection and horror that hysterics profess for them; and he wanted to get them to emit a lethal and completely odorless poison: a fulminating and imperceptible venom. What he intended with this, if anything other than an extravagance, remained forever a mystery to me.

What I found was an old man of simple build who received me with an almost humble courtesy. He was aware of my aspirations, so that we launched at once into a conversation on the topic that brought us together.

He loved his flowers like a father, displaying a fanatic adoration for them. The hypotheses and facts stated above were the introduction to our dialogue; and as the man found in me a fellow expert, he went on to explain in even deeper detail.

After having delineated his theories with rare precision, he invited me to see his violets.

"I have sought," he said as we went along, "to get them, through an evolution of their own nature, to produce venom in their exhalations; and although I have obtained a different result, it corresponds to a real marvel; not to mention that I have not yet given up hope of obtaining the lethal exhalation. But we have arrived; behold them yourself."

They were at the end of the garden, in a kind of small square surrounded by strange plants. Their corollas were jutting out among the normal leaves, and, because of their black color, I at first took them for pansies.

"Black violets!" I exclaimed.

"Yes, indeed; it was necessary to begin with the color, so that the *idea* of death would better engrave itself in them. Black is, except for some Chinese fantasies, the natural color of mourning, for it is the color of night, which is to say of sadness, of the decrease of vitality, and of sleep, which is death's brother. In addition, these flowers do not emit any perfume, as per my design, which is another result produced by the consequences of correlations. Apparently, the color black is, in effect, adverse to perfume; and so it is that of the one thousand, one hundred, and ninety-five species of white flowers, there are seventy-five perfumed and twelve foul-smelling ones; while of the eighteen species of black flowers, there are seventeen odorless and one foul-smelling one. But this is not the interesting part of the affair. The wonder resides in another detail, which requires, unfortunately, a long explanation ..."

"Do not worry," I replied; "my desire to learn is even greater than my curiosity."

"Listen, then, to how I proceeded:

"First of all, I had to furnish my flowers with a medium favorable to the development of ideas of death; then, suggest these ideas to them through a succession of phenomena; followed by having their nervous systems be in such a state that they would be prepared to receive an image and to hold it; and finally, cause the production of the venom by combining, in their surrounding environment and in their sap, diverse vegetable poisons. Heredity would then take care of the rest.

"The violets that you see belong to a family cultivated under that regimen for ten years. Some crossings, indispensable to avoiding degeneration, have forced me to slightly delay the final success of my efforts. And I say the final success, for achieving a black and odorless violet is already a successful result in and of itself.

"But all this was not that difficult; it can be narrowed down to a series of manipulations in which carbon enters as a base with the object of obtaining a variation of indigo. I leave out the details of the investigations about toluidines and xylenes[10] that I was forced to undertake, as their enormously long series would take me far astray, and would also give my secret away. I can give you a clue, however: the source of the color known as indigo is a combination of hydrogen and carbon; the pursuant chemical effort can thus be reduced to securing oxygen and nitrogen, producing the artificial alkali, of which indigo is one type, and afterward obtaining the desired derivatives. I have achieved something similar to this. You are aware that chlorophyll is very sensitive; this explains more than one surprising result. Exposing groups of ivy bushes to sunlight, in a place where the sun came in only through rhomboid openings, I have managed to alter the shape of the ivy leaf—this occurred so persistently, however, that the geometric shape conforms to that of a cissoid curve.[11] Similarly, it does not take much to observe that low grasses in the forest develop in imitation of the arabesques of light that shine through the foliage above . . .

"We arrive now to the main procedure. The suggestion that I try out on my flowers is very difficult to execute, for the brains of the plants are underground: they are inverted beings. Thus I have looked more toward the influence of the medium as the fundamental element. The first funereal note was achieved when I was able to grow the black violets. I then planted around them the vegetables that you see here:

stramonium, jasmine, and belladonna. My violets were thus submitted to funereal influences that are both chemical and physiological. Solanine is, in effect, a narcotic venom; in the same way that daturine contains hyoscyamine and atropine, two pupil-dilating alkaloids that produce megalopsia, or the enlargement of objects. I had, then, the elements of sleep and of hallucinations, which is to say two producers of nightmares; so I had combined this fear to the specific effects of the color black. I must add that to double the impressions of the hallucinations, I also planted henbane, whose radical venom is precisely hyoscyamine."

"And what good is that, given that flowers do not have eyes?" I asked.

"Oh, sir; one does not see only with the eyes," the old man replied. "Somnambulists see with their fingers and with the bottom of their feet. Do not forget that we are dealing here with the power of suggestion."

My lips held back an abundance of objections; but I remained silent, to see how far the development of such a singular theory would take us.

"Solanine and daturine," my interlocutor continued, "are quite similar to the cadaverous poisons ptomaine and leukomaine, which emit the smells of jasmine and of rose. If belladonna and stramonium[12] provide me with these bodies, then the smell can be administered by the jasmine plant and by a rosebush whose perfume I increase, as per an observation by Candolle,[13] by planting onions in its proximity. The cultivation of roses is very advanced now, for large strides have been made with grafts; it was in the time of Shakespeare, after all, that the first rose grafts were introduced in England . . ."

That recollection, clearly meant to flatter my literary inclinations, moved me.

"Allow me," I said, "to express, in passing, admiration at your truly youthful memory."

"To extract even further the influence upon my flowers," he continued, with a vague smile, "I have mixed the cadaverous plants with the narcotic ones. Some arum and orchis, a stapelia here and there, for its smells and colors are reminiscent of rotting flesh. The violets, overexcited by their natural stimulation toward love—given that the flower is a reproductive organ—inhale the perfume of the cadaverous venoms, combined with the smell of the cadaver itself; they suffer the soporific influence of the narcotics, which predisposes them toward hypnosis, and the hallucinatory megalopsia of the pupil-dilating venoms. The suggestion of death thus begins to take effect with all intensity; and yet I increase even further the abnormal sensibility in which the flowers find themselves from their immediacy to those vegetable powers, by occasionally placing close to them shrubs of valerian and field larkspur, whose cyanide irritates them noticeably. The ethylene from the rose also collaborates in this sense. We arrive now at the culminating point in our experiment, but first I must warn you of the following: the human expression *oh!* is a scream from nature."

When I heard this sudden aside, this character's madness became evident to me; without allowing me enough time to even begin to think about this, however, he promptly continued:

"The 'oh!' is, in effect, an interjection of the ages. But the curious thing is that the same occurs among animals. From the dog, a superior vertebrate, to the death's head moth, a butterfly, the 'oh!' is a manifestation of pain and of fear. And precisely this strange insect that I have just mentioned—whose name comes from the fact that it has a skull drawn on its thorax—reminds us at once of the gloomy fauna in which the 'oh!' abounds. It may be unnecessary to mention the horned owl; but we should mention that lost creature from the primitive forests, the sloth, which seems to carry the pain of its decadence in the specific 'oh!' to which he owes one of his names . . .

"And so, exasperated by my ten years of efforts, I decided to perform, in front of the flowers, cruel scenes that would make an even stronger impression upon them, also without success; until one day . . .

". . . But come closer, judge for yourself."

His face was touching the black flowers and, nearly forced to, I did the same. Then—an astonishing thing—I thought I heard a slight moaning. Soon I was convinced. The flowers were uttering slight moans, in effect, as their dark corollas teemed with the emission of little "ohs" quite similar to those of a child. The suggestion had operated in a completely unexpected form, and those flowers, for their entire brief existence, did nothing but cry.

My stupefaction had reached a peak, when I was suddenly overcome by a horrible idea. I remembered that, according to certain legends of black magic, the mandrake also cries when it has been watered with a child's blood; and with a suspicion that made me turn horribly pale, I stood upright.

"Like the mandrake," I said.

"Like the mandrake," he repeated, turning even paler than I.

We never saw each other again. But my conviction now is that he is a true outlaw, a sorcerer from another time, with his venoms and his criminal flowers. Will he finally produce the lethal violet that he seeks? Is it my responsibility to make his evil name public . . . ?

The Pillar of Salt

from *Strange Forces* (1906)

This is how the pilgrim recounted the true story of the monk Sosistrato:

Anyone who has not at some point gone by the monastery of San Sabas must admit that they do not know the meaning of the word desolation. Imagine a very ancient building located above the Jordan, right where the nearly exhausted waters of the river—saturated with yellowish sand—course down toward the Dead Sea through thickets of terebinth trees and apples of Sodom.[1] In that entire area there is but one palm tree, and its crown rises above the walls of the monastery. An infinite solitude, disturbed only on the occasional afternoon by the passing of nomads traveling with their flocks; a colossal silence that seems to descend from the mountains—those eminent mountains that enclose the horizon. When the desert wind blows, an impalpable sand rains down; and when the wind is from the lake, all the plants are covered with salt. Sunset and dawn become confused in the same sadness. Only those who must atone for great crimes would face such solitudes. In the monastery one can hear mass and receive Holy Communion. The monks, of which there are only five left, and all at least sexagenarians, offer the pilgrim a modest meal of fried dates, grapes, water from the river, and sometimes wine from the palm tree. They never leave the monastery, although the neighboring tribes respect them because they are good doctors. When one of them dies, they bury him in the caves below the banks of the river, between the rocks. In these caves, blue doves—friends of the monastery—make their nests in pairs. Before, many years ago already, the first anchorites[2] lived in those caves; one of them was the monk Sosistrato, whose story I have promised to tell you. May Our Lady of Carmelo guide me, and may you listen attentively. What you are about to hear was referred to me word by word by Brother Porphyrius, who is now buried in one of the caves of San Sabas, where his saintly life came to an end, at eighty years of age, in virtue and in penitence. May God have sheltered him in his grace. Amen.

Sosistrato was an Armenian monk who—along with several of his young companions, all recently converted to the religion of Christ—had decided to spend his life in solitude, isolated from worldly life. After a long time roaming through the desert, one day the group found the caverns of which I spoke, and settled there. The water from the Jordan, the fruits from a small garden that they cultivated together, sufficed to meet their needs. They spent their days praying and meditating. Columns of prayers arose from the cracks in

those boulders, and with these efforts, they held up the sway-
ing dome of the heavens, about to collapse upon the sins of
the world. The sacrifices that those exiles made to placate the
just wrath of God, by offering on a daily basis the mortifi-
cation of their flesh and the sorrow of their fasts, avoided
many plagues, wars, and earthquakes. This remains unknown by the impious who laugh lightly at the penitence
of the cenobites.[3] And yet, the sacrifices and the prayers of
the just are the keys that sustain the roof of the universe.

After thirty years of austerity and silence, Sosistrato and
his companions had reached sanctity. The devil, defeated,
wailed in impotence at the feet of the saintly monks. The
lives of the monks slowly came to an end, one after the
other, until finally Sosistrato remained alone. He was very
old, very slight. He had become nearly transparent. He
prayed on his knees fifteen hours a day, and he had revela-
tions. Two friendly doves would bring him a few pomegran-
ate seeds every afternoon and feed him with their beaks. He
lived solely from this; still, he smelled as good as a jasmine
in the afternoon. Every year, when he awoke on the Sorrow of Good Friday, he would find, at the head of his bed
of sticks, a gold cup filled with wine and a loaf of bread;
and with these spices, he would take Holy Communion and
be absorbed in ineffable ecstasy. It never occurred to him
to think where that came from, for he well knew that the
Lord Jesus could provide in this fashion. So he continued
carrying his years, waiting with perfect anointment the day
of his ascension to heavenly bliss. More than fifty years had
passed since a traveler had last gone through there.

But one morning, while the monk was praying with his
doves, the birds became suddenly frightened and took flight,
abandoning him. A pilgrim had arrived at the entrance to
the cavern. Sosistrato, after greeting him with saintly words,

invited him to rest, pointing toward a pitcher of water. The stranger drank anxiously, as if overcome with exhaustion; and after eating a handful of dried fruits that he took out of his knapsack, he prayed alongside the monk.

Seven days went by. The traveler recounted his pilgrimage from Caesarea[4] to the shores of the Dead Sea, concluding his narrative with a story that worried Sosistrato.

"I have seen the corpses of the accursed cities," he said to his host one night; "I have seen the sea smoking like a furnace, and—full of terror—I have set eyes upon the woman of salt, the wife of Lot, punished.[5] The woman is alive, my brother; I have heard her moaning and have seen her perspiring in the noontime sun."

"Juvencus tells of something similar in his treaty *De Sodom*,"[6] Sosistrato said in a low voice.

"Yes, I know the passage," the pilgrim added. "There is certainly something definitive about it; for it turns out that Lot's wife has continued to be alive as a woman, physiologically. And I thought that it would be a good deed of charity to free her from her sentence . . ."

"It is the justice of God," the solitary man exclaimed.

"Did Christ not also come to redeem the sins of the ancient world with his sacrifice?" the traveler, who seemed learned in sacred letters, replied softly. "Does baptism not equally wash away sins against the Law as well as sins against the Gospels . . . ?"

After these words, both men fell asleep. That was the last night they spent together. The next day the stranger departed, taking Sosistrato's blessings with him . . . And it should not be necessary to tell you that, despite his good appearances, the false pilgrim was Satan himself.

The evil one's project was subtle. From that night on, a tenacious preoccupation struck the spirit of the saintly monk.

To baptize the pillar of salt, to free that trapped spirit from its torment! Charity demanded it, reason argued for it. The monk spent months struggling with this until at last he had a vision. An angel appeared to him in his dreams and ordered him to carry out the act.

Sosistrato prayed and fasted for three days, and on the morning of the fourth day, leaning on his acacia staff, he set out along the edge of the Jordan on the path toward the Dead Sea. The journey was not long, but his tired legs could barely hold him up. He walked in this manner for two days. The faithful doves continued to feed him as always, and he prayed often and very deeply, for his resolution had him extremely distressed. Finally, when his legs were about to fail him, the mountains parted and the lake appeared.

The skeletons of the destroyed cities had been slowly fading. A few burnt boulders were all that was left by now: fragments of arches, rows of clay bricks consumed by the salt and covered with bitumen.[7] . . . The monk barely heeded these residues, trying merely to avoid them so that his feet would not become stained by stepping on them. All of a sudden, his old body trembled from top to bottom. He had just seen, toward the south, beyond the rubble, in a bend in the mountains that was not usually visible, the silhouette of the pillar.

Beneath its petrified mantle—worn away by time—she was long and thin as a ghost. The sun shone with a clear incandescence, burning the stones and turning the brackish layer that covered the leaves of the terebinth trees into glaring reflectors. Beneath the meridian reflection, the shrubs seemed to be made of silver. There was not a single cloud in the sky. The bitter waters slept in their characteristic immobility. According to the pilgrims, the moaning of the specters of the Cities of the Plain could be heard in those waters when the wind blew.

Sosistrato approached the pillar. The traveler had spoken truthfully. A warm moisture covered its face. Its white eyes and white lips were completely motionless in the centuries-long sleep beneath the invasion of the stone. Not a single sign of life emanated from the rock. The sun glared down upon it with implacable tenacity, always the same for thousands of years; and yet, the effigy was alive, for it was perspiring! This very sleep summed up the mysteries of biblical horrors. Would it not be reckless to attempt to disturb such sleep? Would the sin of the damned woman not fall upon the senseless man who sought to redeem her? To awaken such a mystery was criminal madness, perhaps an infernal temptation. Sosistrato, full of anguish, kneeled down in the shadow of a thicket to pray . . .

How the action came to pass, I shall not tell you. Know only that when the sacramental water fell upon the pillar, the salt slowly dissolved, and before the solitary man's eyes a woman appeared, as old as eternity, covered in tattered rags, with an ashen lividness, thin and trembling, full of centuries. The monk, who had looked upon the devil without fear, was terrified at the sight of this apparition. He saw the reprobates rising with her. Those eyes had seen the combustion of brimstone—driven by divine rage—raining down upon the infamy of the Cities of the Plain; those rags were woven with the hair of the camels of Lot; those feet had tread upon the ashes of the fire of the Eternal One! Then the frightening woman spoke to him in her ancient voice.

She no longer remembered anything. Only a vague vision of the fire, a dark sensation brought to life at the sight of that sea. Her soul was covered in confusion. She had slept for a long time, a black sleep like that of the grave. She suffered without knowing why, submerged in that nightmare. The monk had just saved her. She felt it. It was the only clear thing in her recent vision. And the sea . . . the fire . . . the catastrophe . . . the burning cities . . . all that faded in a clear vision of death. She was going to die. She was saved, then. And the monk had saved her!

Sosistrato was trembling, formidably. A red flame burned in his pupils. The past faded from him, as if a wind of fire had swept through his soul. And only one thought occupied his consciousness: *Lot's wife was right there in front of him!* The sun was setting behind the mountains, staining the horizon with a fiery purple. The tragic days of times past were relived in the show of flames. It was like a resurrection of the punishment, reflected for a second time upon the waters of the bitter lake. Sosistrato had just gone back through the centuries. He remembered. He had played a role in the catastrophe. And this woman . . . he knew this woman!

Then a horrible anguish burned his flesh. His tongue spoke, directing itself toward the resuscitated specter:

"Woman, answer me just one thing."

"Speak . . . ask . . ."

"Will you answer?"

"Yes, speak; you have saved me!"

The eyes of the anchorite glowed, reflecting the very radiance burning behind the mountains.

"Woman, tell me what you saw when you turned around to look."[8]

A voice knotted in anguish responded:

"Oh, no . . . For the sake of Elohim,[9] do not ask me that!"

"Tell me what you saw!"

"No . . . no . . . That would mean the abyss!"

"I want the abyss."

"That would mean certain death . . ."

"Tell me what you saw!"

"I cannot . . . I will not!"

"I have saved you."

"No . . . no . . ."

The sun had just set.

"Speak!"

The woman went closer to him. Her voice seemed to be covered in dust, fading, setting, agonizing.

"For the sake of your parents' ashes . . . !"

"Speak!"

Then the specter put her mouth to the cenobite's ear, and spoke one word. And Sosistrato, struck down, fell dead, without exclaiming a single sound. Let us pray to God for his soul.

The Escuerzo[1]

from *Strange Forces* (1906)

One day like any other, playing outside the family country house, I found a small toad that, instead of escaping like his more corpulent fellows, swelled up in an extraordinary fashion when I tried to stone him. Toads horrified me and I often amused myself by squashing as many of them as I could. So it was not long before the small, stubborn reptile collapsed under the blows of my stones. Like all boys raised in the semi-rural life of our provincial cities, I was an expert in lizards and toads. Furthermore, our house was located near a creek that crossed the city, which helped increase the frequency of my encounters with such creatures. I go into these details so that my surprise at noticing that the peevish little toad was entirely unknown to me will be better understood. A circumstance for a consultation, this was. And taking my victim with all the precaution the case deserved, I went to ask the old servant about it, confident in my first undertakings as a hunter. I was eight years of age and she sixty. The affair was, in effect, to interest us both. The good woman was sitting at the kitchen door as usual, and I expected to see my story received with her customary goodwill; but as soon as I began to recount it, she quickly got up and seized the small animal from my hands, its insides hanging out.

"Thank God that you did not leave it behind!" she exclaimed, with an expression of utmost relief. "We will go burn it this very instant."

"Burn it?" I said; "but what good will that do, if it is already dead . . ."

"Don't you know that this frog is an *escuerzo*," my interlocutor replied in a mysterious tone, "and that this little animal will come back to life if it is not burned? Who told you to kill it! That is what comes at last from you always throwing rocks at animals! Now I will tell you what happened to the son of my friend the late Antonia, may she rest in peace."

As she spoke, she gathered and lighted some kindling, and then placed upon it the body of the horned frog.

"An *escuerzo*!" I said, my young, mischievous flesh crawling with terror; "an *escuerzo*!" And I shook my fingers as if the toad's cold had stuck to them. "A toad that comes back to life!" That would have chilled the bones of a fully bearded man, not to mention those of a boy.

"But are you about to tell us a new Batrachomyomachy?"[2] Julia interrupted at this point, with the friendly, coquettish ease of her thirty years of age.

"Not at all, miss. It is a story that *really* happened."

Julia smiled.

"You cannot imagine how much I would like to hear it . . ."

"And so you shall, all the more so because it is my intention to avenge your smile with it."

This, then, is how we proceeded, my fateful hunted item burning as the old servant wove the following narrative:

Antonia, her friend, a soldier's widow, lived in a very poor, small house, far from any town, with her only son by her late husband. The lad worked for both of them, cutting wood in the nearby forest, and in this fashion year after year passed, as they made their way through life's journey. One day he returned in the afternoon, as usual, to drink his *mate*,[3] happy, healthy, energetic, with his axe over his shoulder. And while they were preparing the *mate*, he reported to his mother that on the root of a certain very old tree he had found an *escuerzo*, which, puff his chest out as he might, ended up flat as a tortilla under the shaft of his axe.

The poor old lady, overcome with distress upon hearing this, asked him to please accompany her to the spot, so they could burn the animal's body at once.

"You should know," she told him, "that an *escuerzo* never forgives the one who offends him. If it is not burned, it comes back to life, it follows his murderer's trail, and does not rest until it is able to harm him in kind."

The good lad laughed loudly at the story, trying to convince the poor old woman that that was a good tall tale to frighten troublesome children, but that it should not worry people of a certain intelligence. She insisted, however, that he accompany her to burn the remains of the horned frog.

All jokes, every indication about how far the place was, about the harm that the November evening dew might cause her, she being already so old—all this was futile. She wished to go at all costs and he eventually consented to accompany her.

The distance was not that great, six blocks or so at the most. Easily they found the recently chopped tree, but no matter how much they searched among the twigs and the scattered branches, the body of the *escuerzo* did not appear.

"Did I not tell you?" she exclaimed, and burst out crying; "it has already left; now there is nothing we can do. May Saint Anthony protect you!"

"How silly, to get so upset. The ants must have taken it away, or some hungry fox must have eaten it. Has anyone ever seen such extravagance, to cry over a toad! The best thing to do is to go back, as nightfall is approaching and the dew from the grasses is harmful."

So they returned to their little house, she crying the entire time, he seeking to distract her with details about the field of corn, which promised a good harvest if the rains kept up; until he once again joked and laughed before her obstinate sadness. It was nearly nighttime when they arrived. After a detailed search of all the corners, nooks, and crannies, which once again caused the lad to laugh, they ate outside on the patio, silently, under the moonlight; and he was already preparing to lie down on his saddle to go to sleep, when Antonia begged him, at least for that one night, to consent to locking himself inside a wooden box of hers, and to sleep there.

The lad's protest against such a request was lively. She was behaving like a doddering old fool, there was no doubt about it. Who would think of making him sleep, with that heat, inside a box that was probably full of bugs!

But such were the old woman's pleas that, since the lad loved her so, he decided to consent to her extravagant whim. The box was large, and although a bit tight, he would not be all that badly off. His bedding was arranged at the bottom with great attention, he got inside, and the sad widow took a seat next to the item of furniture, her mind made up to spend the entire night awake, so she could close the box at the first sign of danger.

She calculated that it must be around midnight, for the moon was starting to bathe the room with her light, when all of a sudden a small, black, nearly imperceptible shape jumped on the threshold of the door, which had been left open because of the tremendous heat. Antonia trembled with anguish.

There it was, then, the vengeful animal, sitting on its rear legs, as if it were devising a plan. How mistaken the lad had been to laugh! That small, wretched shape, resting motionless at the fully moonlit door, seemed to grow in an extraordinary fashion and to take on the dimensions of a monster. But, what if it was nothing other than one of the many familiar toads that came in every night in search of insects? She breathed for a moment, sustained by this idea. But the *escuerzo* suddenly took a little jump, then another, in the direction of the box. Its intentions were manifest. It did not hurry, as if it were certain of its prey. Antonia looked at her son with an unspeakable expression of terror; he was sleeping, overcome by fatigue, breathing rhythmically.

Then, with an uncertain hand, she silently dropped the lid on the heavy item of furniture. The animal did not stop. It kept on hopping. It was already at the foot of the box. It circled it deliberately, stopped at one of its angles, and, all of a sudden, with an incredible jump for its small size, landed on top of the box.

Antonia did not dare to make the slightest movement. At that moment her whole life came together before her. The moon now illuminated the room entirely. And here is what happened: the toad began to swell incrementally, it grew, it grew in a prodigious manner, until it was three times its weight. It remained like that for a minute, during which time the poor woman felt all the affliction of death weigh down upon her heart. Then it shrank down, shrinking down until it recovered its original shape; it hopped down to the ground, headed toward the door, and, crossing the patio, eventually faded into the grass.

Finally Antonia dared to get up, shaking all over. With a violent gesture she tore open the box. What she felt was so horrendous that a few months later she also died, a victim of the fright produced in her at that moment.

A deadly cold rose out of the open box; under the sad light in which the moon shrouded the sepulchral remains, the lad lay frozen and stiff, already turned to stone under an inexplicable bath of frost.

The Horses of Abdera[1]

from *Strange Forces* (1906)

Abdera, the Thracian city of the Aegean—also known now as Balastra,[2] and not to be confused with its Baetican namesake[3]—was renowned for its horses.

To stand out in Thrace for one's horses was no small feat; and Abdera not only stood out for her horses, she was considered unique because of them. The inhabitants all took pride in the education of such a noble animal; and this passion, cultivated insistently over long years until it formed a fundamental aspect of the city's traditions, had produced marvelous effects. The horses of Abdera enjoyed exceptional fame, and residents of all Thracian towns, from the Cicones to the Bisaltos, paid tribute in this to the Bistones,[4] the inhabitants of the aforementioned city. It should be added that this industry, which combined profit with satisfaction, occupied everyone, beginning with the king and extending to the very last citizen.

These circumstances also contributed to making the relationships between the beasts and their owners more intimate, much more so than what was and what is common for other nations. Thus, the stables were considered an expansion of one's inner home; and this passion, taken to an extreme through the natural processes of exaggeration, drove the inhabitants of Abdera as far as having them admit their horses to dine at the table with them.

Although they were still beasts, they were truly admirable steeds. Some slept under byssus[5] bedspreads, while some mangers were decorated with simple frescos, for more than a few veterinarians upheld the artistic taste of the equine race. And the horse cemetery boasted, mostly among undoubtedly overdecorated bourgeois ostentations, two or three real masterpieces. The most beautiful temple in the city was consecrated to Arion, the horse that Neptune brought to bear from the ground with a blow of his trident,[6] and I believe that the fashion of placing heads of horses on the ends of prows comes from this same origin—it being certain, in any case, that equine bas-reliefs were the most common decorations in all of Abdera's architecture. Furthermore, the monarch was the most demonstratively on the side of the steeds, even tolerating actual crimes from his horses. This of course made the horses extraordinarily wild, to such an extent that the names of Podargos and of Lampon[7] figured in gloomy fables—for I should add that these horses had names, just like people.

So tame were these animals that bridles were unnecessary, and these were kept on simply as decorations, much valued in fact by the horses themselves. Words were the usual means of communicating with them; and observing that liberty favored the development of their good conditions, they were allowed to roam at all times without pack-saddles or harnesses, free to cross as they pleased, for their pleasure and nourishment, to the magnificent prairies in the surrounding environs, at the edge of the Kossinites River.[8]

When they were needed they were called with the sound of blowing trumpets, and be it for work or to feed, they would respond at once. Their skills at all manner of circus, and even salon, games verged on the incredible, as did their bravery in battle and their discretion in solemn ceremonies. Thus, Abdera's hippodrome, as well as its acrobatic companies, its bronze-armored cavalry and its burials, had gained such renown that people came to see them from far and wide. The credit was due equally to the trainers and the steeds.

This persistent education, this forced unfolding of conditions, and, in a word, this *humanization* of the equine race, began to engender a phenomenon that the Bistones celebrated as another national glory: the intelligence of their horses began to develop on pace with their consciousness, producing abnormal cases that fed the flames of daily conversations.

A mare had demanded mirrors for her manger, ripping them out from her owner's own alcove with her teeth, and kicking and destroying those from three other panels when her wishes were not granted. When her whim was granted, she displayed perfectly identifiable gestures of coquetry.

Balios, the most beautiful colt in the region, a white, elegant, and sentimental horse who had served in two military campaigns and who showed delight at the recital of heroic hexameters, had just died of love for a lady. She was the wife of the owner of the infatuated beast, a general who, it should be noted, did not hide the occurrence. On the contrary, he felt that it praised his vanity—the latter being quite a natural trait in the equestrian metropolis.

Likewise, there were reports of horse infanticide, and as these were increasing at an alarming rate, it became necessary to introduce old adoptive mules, their presence serving as a force of prevention. The horses also developed a growing taste for fish and hemp and the animals had begun to pillage the plantations of the latter. And there were several isolated rebellions that—the whip proving to be insufficient—had to be controlled with burning iron. This last occurrence was on the rise, however, for the instinct toward rebellion progressed despite everything else.

But the Bistones, more enchanted than ever with their horses, did not stop to think for very long about all this. Still, other, more significant events soon occurred. Two or three teams of horses came together against the driver of a wagon who was whipping his rebellious mare. Horses overall began resisting the harness and the yoke more and more all the time, to the point that donkeys came to be preferred for many tasks. And there were animals that did not accept certain riding gear; but because they belonged to the wealthy, their rebellion was considered somehow different and was referred to fondly as a caprice.

One day the horses did not come at the blowing of the trumpets, and it was necessary to constrain them by force; but the rebellion did not occur on the following day.

Finally the rebellion did occur, one day that the tide covered the beach with dead fishes, as it often did. The horses were fed up with this; they were seen returning to the fields outside the city with a somber slowness.

The extraordinary conflict erupted at midnight.

All of a sudden a deafening and persistent thundering shook the entire city. It was the horses, all of them together moving to attack the city; but this was known only later, for it went unobserved at first in the darkness of night and the surprise of the unexpected.

As the prairies used for pasture were within the walls, there was nothing to slow the attack; this, combined with the minute knowledge that the animals had of the houses in the city, greatly increased the level of the catastrophe.

The most memorable of nights, its horrors became apparent only when they were revealed at dawn, at which point the morning light multiplied them even further.

The kicked-down doors lay on the ground, having given way to one ferocious stampede after another, almost without interruption. Blood had run, for more than a few residents had fallen, crushed under the hooves and the teeth of the packs of horses, amid which human weapons also wreaked havoc.

Shaken by the multitudes, the city had darkened with the dust that had been kicked up; and a strange uproar—composed of screams of anger or of pain; of neighs, as varied as words, mixed with some anguished braying or another; and of the stomping on doors and partitions—added its horror to the visible terror of the catastrophe. A kind of incessant earthquake made the ground tremble with the trotting of the rebellious mass, exalted at times like a bursting hurricane by frantic throngs without direction or purpose; for having plundered all the fields of hemp, and even some bodegas coveted by those steeds perverted by the refinements of the dining table, groups of drunken animals accelerated the work of destruction. And escape by sea was also impossible, for the horses, knowing about the use of ships, had closed off all access to the port.

Only the fortress remained intact, and a resistance began to be organized there. For the time being any horse that passed in front of it was riddled with arrows; and when it fell nearby, it was dragged inside for provisions.

The strangest of rumors circulated among the residents who had taken refuge in the fortress. The first attack had been merely a pillaging, some said. Once the doors were knocked down, the packs flocked into the rooms, focused solely on the splendid tapestries, with which they attempted to dress themselves, and on the jewelry and other bright objects. Any opposition to their intentions aroused their fury.

Others spoke of monstrous loves, of women accosted and crushed on their own beds under a bestial impetus. And there was even a noble maiden who, crying, recounted her misfortune of two crises: first, being awoken in her bed, her lamp dimly lit, her lips grazed by the ignoble face of a black colt curling its lips excitedly, showing its horrible set of teeth, and her scream of terror before that animal-become-beast, as she saw an evil, human glow in its eyes, burning with lewdness; and second, the sea of blood in which the beast flooded her when it fell, pierced by a servant's sword ...

Several killings were recounted in which the mares had taken pleasure, with female fury, at crushing and biting their victims. The donkeys had been exterminated, and the mules rebelled as well, but with an unconscious awkwardness, destroying for the sake of destruction, and particularly set against the dogs.

The thundering of the maddened races continued to shake the city, and the uproar of collapsing structures increased. If the city was not to be abandoned to the most senseless destruction, it was urgent to organize a way out, even though the number and the strength of the attackers made it singularly dangerous.

The men began to arm themselves. Soon after the first moments of wantonness, the horses also decided to attack the fortress.

An abrupt silence preceded the assault. From the fortress people could make out the terrible army congregating, not without some effort, at the hippodrome. This took several hours, for when everything appeared to be ready, sudden bucks and very sharp neighs, whose cause it was impossible to discern, would thoroughly disorganize the ranks.

The sun was already setting when the first charge was produced. It was, if I may say so, merely a demonstration, for the animals limited themselves to running by the fortress. They were, however, riddled by the defenders' arrows.

From the furthest edges of the city, they surged again, and their clash against the defenses was formidable. The entire fortress trembled under a tempest of hooves, and its robust Doric walls were left deeply damaged, if truth be told.

They were turned back, but this was followed very quickly by a new attack.

Horses and branded mules fell by the dozen, but their ranks closed with a furious bloodthirstiness, and their numbers did not seem to diminish. Making matters worse was the fact that some animals had managed to dress themselves in combat armor, so that the arrows were deflected by their steel mail. Some wore shreds of colorful cloth, others necklaces; and acting simultaneously childish and enraged, they would perform unexpected frolicky jumps.

People recognized them from the walls: Dinos, Aethon, Ameteo, Xanthos! And they, in turn, greeted those in the fortress, neighing delightedly, arching their tails, charging at once with fiery starts. One, clearly a leader, rose up on its hindquarters, walked for a stretch like this, pawing gallantly at the air as if it were dancing a martial waltz, curving its neck with serpentine elegance, until an arrow pierced it in the middle of its chest . . .

Meanwhile, the attackers were prevailing. The walls were beginning to give way.

All of a sudden an alarm froze the creatures. One against the other, leaning on each other's croups and backs, they stretched their necks toward the promenade that bordered the edge of the Kossinites River. The defenders in the fortress turned in the same direction and witnessed a tremendous spectacle.

Above the black trees and against the afternoon sky, the terrifying, colossal head of a lion had appeared, looking toward the city. It was an antediluvian beast, one of those specimens that, more rarely all the time, would occasionally devastate the Rhodope Mountains.[9] But nothing as monstrous as this had ever been seen: the head of the colossal lion stood high above the tallest trees, the twilight-tainted leaves brushing against the tangled locks of its mane.

Its eyes could be seen squinting before the light, its enormous fangs shining clearly; its wild smell reached them with the blowing breeze. Motionless in the waving foliage, bronzed by the sun so that its gigantic mane seemed to be made of gold, it rose against the horizon like one of those blocks out of which the Pelasgians,[10] their contemporaries from the mountains, sculpted their barbaric divinities.

And suddenly it began to walk, as slow as the ocean. They heard the branches being pushed out of its way by its chest; they also heard its furnace breath, which would doubtlessly shake the city whenever the lion decided to roar.

Despite their prodigious force and numbers, the rebelling horses did not attempt to resist the approaching creature. As if driven by a unified force, they headed toward the beach, in the direction of Macedonia, raising a veritable hurricane of sand and foam, more than a few of them shooting off through the waves.

A sense of panic reigned in the fortress. What could they do against such an enemy? What bronze hinge could resist its mandibles? What wall hold back its claws . . . ?

They were already starting to think that they preferred the previous danger (at least that had been a battle against civilized animals), and they had not even the will to draw their bows against this one, when the monster stepped out of the grove.

What then erupted from its fauces was not a roar, but a human war scream—the bellicose *alalé* of battles, to which they replied from the fortress, with joyful triumph, the *hoyohei* and the *hoyotohó*.

Glorious wonder!

Under the feline's head, a superior light glowed from the face of a numen;[11] his marmoreal chest, oaken arms, and stupendous thighs stood out and combined superbly with his honey-colored skin.

And a shout, a single shout of liberty, of recognition, of pride, filled the afternoon:

"Hercules, Hercules has come!"

Essays, Addresses,
and Nonfiction

This Country's Politicians II[1]
from *La montaña* (1897)

The term of the presidency of the republic is about to come to an end, and the public conscience has expressed with eloquent unanimity its judgment of the citizen who currently holds the post. And the judgment is pronounced as follows: Uriburu[2] is a useless old man, a poor old man, a fungus transplanted and stuck onto the leg of the presidential chair, sprouting there by chance, or perhaps in passivity—as this tends to be, in Argentina, a not insignificant path to political triumph, as well as a good indication of cheap prostitution.

José Evaristo Uriburu is a politician without a biography, or perhaps a biography without a character. He was sent to Chile with the credentials of a minister, and he spent years and years there, like so many others, letting the world spin round and round, and gobbling up his diplomatic salary—which is, after all, why they were giving it to him: so he would gobble it up.

One day it was necessary to bring to the vice presidency of the republic a docile servant, one capable of holding his laughter in the presence of other signs, and even of taking seriously the prebends[3] and the attributions contained in that dirty paper known as the constitution. The country heard with surprise the name of José Evaristo, prescribed to it like any other bitter pill, and with its good sense, as always, the country said to itself that José Evaristo, as an unknown, would not necessarily eat more than any other man named just José or Evaristo. And the country accepted him with as much reason as any, for it was not the one electing him.

The old Sáenz Peña[4] fell silently, like a snail, without making a single sound, and the gelatinous president was replaced by a vice president of cotton.

Since then he is there where they have put him, waiting to be removed. It is already resolved that he will be given a senatorship when he leaves the presidency. And nothing more.

He has had one virtue, or rather something that in his class is considered a virtue, according to what the bourgeois press will have us hear every day: he has not stolen. And effectively so; this is one of the major things that a republican functionary can accomplish. Stealing is so deeply rooted in the customs of the wealthy classes that being inept at being a thief is considered a precious and rare gift. But understand clearly: It is not the capacity to not be a thief, but the ineptitude of being one.

And so, for example, they say that Roca[5] will not steal in the future presidency because he is already very rich. This is a political calculation in the most genuine of bourgeois molds. In order not to steal, it is necessary to already have stolen—to the point of saturation. These are the resulting morals of those who undertake pilgrimages to Luján[6] and send their children to Jesuit boarding schools. And the fortune of the people resides in the hands of such individuals. So what else do the upper classes, *the decent people*, deserve from us other than contempt and disgust? Everywhere the slaughter of pigs tends to signify a feast. So much pork in the upper classes . . . !

But the working classes are still sufficiently foolish to limit themselves to envying their luxuries, banquets, and women. And this even though it would suffice for them to look at their own hands to become aware of their abilities. A few thousand individuals—wasted by their excessive indulgence, imbeciles to the last degree of ineptitude, ignorant in everything that might be of major importance or beauty, or even simply of honesty—exploit, tyrannize, abuse, insult with their stolen ostentations the misery of many millions of strong men, who would only need a little push to drive that rotted mass to Hell. With the law in their hands? No. With bare-knuckled fists.

The law, with those who are lawless, with those who write it with the blade of a saber? The law, with those who swindle or commit crimes, even among each other, as they contend for control of the press? Much would they like this, so as to laugh once again at the idiots who continue believing in the republican farce, despite being its victims. No!

It is just for citizens, it is just and honorable for them to avoid the law, to laugh at the constitution and to defend themselves from fraud when fraud seeks to squash them. Today, everything related to destroying the social order is sacred; and breaking the law nearly equates to fighting for one's emancipation. That is what the example of the upper classes teaches us; the more they violate the law, the freer they feel. Let us take advantage of the lesson. Let us violate it as well. And when they come to take account of our actions with the threat of brute force, let us oppose force with force; and then we will see if it is so difficult to cast a congress according to Norwegian custom: down from the balconies. You say that some representative will be smashed against the stones? Bah! There are so many skinny dogs that have an indisputable right to live! And the bones of our compatriots have appeased the hunger of so many dogs in the fields of battle!

As far as José Evaristo Uriburu is concerned, I confess, quite frankly, that I no longer find anything to say about him. There is a certain candor in stupidity, impervious to any acid. A certain class of members of the bourgeoisie, *well-respected men*, have that candor. Imbecile or idler: these are the terms of the bourgeois intelligentsia. For either one they are venerated with a statue. And quite often, after all, the pedestal of the statue serves as a urinal for the riffraff. President Uriburu will not have a statue. The liquid excrement of the miserable shall never splash upon him. But this is because he will not have a statue.

The Morality of Art

from *La montaña* (1897)

It is not possible to make two-faced art. That would be an indignity, something akin to casually kissing one's sleeping mother.

However, because there are swine in art, too, one would do well to be careful. To make great and productive art, to mold mountains and to be able to put one's hands on the harp of the tempest, one must be possessed by a single idea, an idea that should also be a passion: an anger, a love, a melancholy, a hatred, *something*: the thunderstorm of Isaiah or the little *ah!* accepted by the indulgence of the heavens.

Faith, above all, a faith as ardent, as alive, as tumultuous as blood; mad faith, angry faith, compassionate faith, unrestrained faith, cruel faith, bright faith, humble faith, but always as firm as the neck musculature of a bull.

After that, one must have sincerity, a virtue found in every star. Sincerity can be acquired in one of two ways: through innocence or through contempt. The latter is virile sincerity. In order to manifest itself, only two things are required: solitude and pride: characters distinctive of every summit.

Any artist who believes himself to be one, who accepts the terrible task of being one of God's missionaries, must renounce all lowly embarrassment, and above all the conventional scruples of social mores. The artist, like nature, does not know shyness. Even more: he does not need it for anything. Only the vulgar and bad souls of "good people" have any need for crutches. The man who is truly free must be violently free, and the concept of idealism leaves no room for doubt. If the world is nothing more than an exteriorized objectification of my *I*, it is clear that I have the absolute right to transform it in my own way. If the harmony that results as a consequence of the different objectifications—the synthesis of which gives me an idea of the world—does not satisfy me today, I shall abandon it immediately. For I have only one morality, my own, totally diverse from that of everyone else. Its logic is inside myself and I am the only one who can change it. Hence the negation of any embarrassment before society. Small spirits, unable to put up with the ebb tide of this large moveable water that is consciousness, find themselves very comfortable in the servitude of reading primers, in the harness of schools and canons. That is how I understand the bliss of the beast. And men generally tend, with an irresistible impulse, toward those embarrassing nullifications of the *I*. What most bothers vulgar people is non-conformism. The expression of such discomfort is idiotically monotonous: *madness! He is mad!* It has always been the same, from the beginnings of the world, because the bourgeoisie has been present in every period of time. The ox has always ruminated in the same way, the ass has always kicked in the same manner, the bourgeoisie has always thought the same things. Even worse: it is fatally condemned to always think the same things. There is only one exception to this: when it cannot think anymore, it digests. Hence the irrepressible passion of vulgar men for their characteristic perpetuity: eternal morality, eternal religion, eternal property, eternal commerce, eternal imbecility. All of it charming for people of homeopathic thinking; the triumph of the most complete intellectual unreceptiveness; the true concept of a megathere[1] brimming with herbivore health.

The artist must revolt against all of this and proclaim the most intransigent of Neronian intellectualisms.[2] To the best of my knowledge, the most eloquent way to protest against all of this is to be cruel toward the obtuse. Within the current state of social affairs, nothing reveals one's personality as much as abuse and, better yet, tyranny. Hence the tendency of tyrants to fatten their buffoons. We intellectuals are luckier than political despots, because we have buffoons fattened at their own expense. This type is called a "decent gentleman."

This animal, admirably organized for perpetual swallowing, must be the object of all our cruelties. The kingdom of his bestiality is just. The attack must thus be against what is just. If not, we will remain spinning through the end of the centuries in the vileness of normality.

We must at all costs get out of the uniforms in which we have been packed by a row of men. At the pace at which we are proceeding, and if we do not place any limitations on the degrading modesty of the bourgeoisie, before too long it will be an offense to go around with one's nose uncovered. It is true that hermetic underpants hide, quite admirably, many pederasties and many epigastric hyperboles. But enough already of bashful underskirts, of cotton modesty and of cashmere shyness!

We, we do not want girdles.

Prologue to the First Edition of Lunario Sentimental *(Sentimental Lunarium)*

1909

Fortunately, the time of having to apologize to practical people for writing verse is coming to an end.

Finally, so many of us have written that the aforementioned individuals are having to tolerate our whim.

But this gracious concession only encourages us to attempt something even more necessary, albeit more difficult: to demonstrate, to those same practical people, the utility of verse for the cultivation of the language. For regardless what minimum importance one concedes to this organism, no one will fail to recognize—given that we all need to speak in language—the advantage one has when one is able to speak clearly and with brevity.

By definition, because of the forced limitation imposed by its meter, verse is concise, and it must be clear to be pleasing. This latter is an abundantly important condition, for the ultimate end of verse is to please.

As it is concise and clear, verse tends to be definitive, and thus contributes new proverbial expressions or ready-made phrases that save the tongue time and effort—a precious quality for those practical people. Suffice it to recall the octosyllabic structure of nearly all adages.[1]

As time passes, and without practical people noticing it, such expressions degenerate into commonplaces. But such a vice can be mended in the following way: since verse lives off of metaphor, which is to say from the picturesque analogy among things themselves, it requires new phrases to expound said analogies—if it is to be original, as it should be.

Furthermore, language is a set of images, consisting, if one looks at it properly, of one metaphor per word; therefore, finding new, beautiful images, and expressing them with clarity and concision, is a way of simultaneously enriching and renovating the language. Those in charge of this labor—which is at least as honorable as that of refining livestock or administering the public debt, given that it serves a social function—are the poets. Language is a public good; even more, it is a nation's most solid element.

The commonplace is bad, as it eventually loses all meaning of expression through its excessive usage. Originality cures this inconvenience, as it thinks up new concepts requiring new expressions. Thus, verse coins the most useful expressions because it is the most concise and clear, renovating said expressions through the same process as when it purifies a commonplace.

In addition, verse is one of the fine arts, and it is well known that cultivation of the fine arts civilizes the people.

Practical individuals count this truth as one of their fundamental notions.

When a person who considers himself to be cultured says that he does not perceive the charm of verse, he is revealing a relative un-refinement, which does no harm to verse, of course. Homer, Dante, Hugo will always be greater than that person, simply because they composed verse; and certainly that person would love to be in their place.

Disdaining verse is like not appreciating painting or music. It is a phenomenon characteristic of lack of culture.

It is also a mistake to believe that verse is not very practical.

On the contrary, it is as practical as any work of luxury can be. Someone who pays for an elegant drawing room, or a subscription to the opera, or a beautiful tomb, or a grand mansion pays the same tribute to the fine arts as someone who acquires a book of good verse. Luxury is the name given to the purchase and possession of works produced by the fine arts.

There is no difference, other than the lower cost of the book, between the latter and the drawing room or the theater box; but practical people no longer ignore that it is a vulgarity to question the price of works in the fine arts. The process of acquiring books of beauty will be the same as how one satisfies one's cult of luxury in architecture, painting, sculpture, and music.

Why should poetry not be the Cinderella among them, for in its power one finds, precisely, the crystal slipper . . . ?

I warn you, furthermore, that I consider myself a practical man. I am thirty-four years of age . . . and I have lived.

I owe a word also to the men of letters, with regard to the free verse that I use in abundance in the pages that follow.[2]

As its name indicates, free verse signifies something simple and grand: the conquering of a freedom.

Prose reaches it completely, although its paragraphs follow a rhythm that is as predetermined as strophes.

There was a time, however—the great time of Cicero—when Latin oratory used famous metric clauses to flatter the ear of the listener, composing endings out of propositions and phrases, in successive rhythmic feet. The objective of these was precisely to avoid, at the endings, the rhythm of common verses, such as hexameters, pentameters, dactyls—although others were eventually adopted in their place, such as the three-syllabled foot or the *amphimacers* mentioned by the sublime orator.[3,4]

The audience demanded the observance of these metric clauses, which had been decreed in this manner since the time of Cicero. Pliny assures us that he even verified them by measuring them to the rhythm of his pulse: to such an extent did the ear find itself capable of perceiving them. Although it is true that, in Latin, the nature of the language is that it produces metric clauses of its own accord in the middle of phrases.

Naturally, verses and strophes follow this very same nature, but their selective success or triumph cannot mean, by any means, that they become exclusive.

But triumphant forms tend to exclude other forms; and thus, to liberate Latin prose from the aforementioned Ciceronian clauses, it was necessary for Caesar himself—liberator of so many things—to revolt, as did Varro and Cornelius Nepos as well.[5]

Our classical verses, before becoming classical, had to battle in their media like all organisms that are to survive. The history of the hendecasyllable, as Jaimes Freyre recounts in his outstanding study on Spanish verse,[6] is a perfect example. When it was first introduced from Italy, many men of letters in Spain did not accept the hendecasyllable, arguing that it was unharmonious. The octosyllable itself, seemingly so natural, wavers and stumbles in the earliest *romances . . .*[7]

What we call free verse, and which of course is not *blank* or rhymeless verse, as the Spanish rhetoricians call it, attends primarily to the harmonious ensemble of the strophe, subordinating the rhythm of each member, so that the strophe may thus have a more varied result.

Furthermore, in this manner, the result is a more united strophe, with rhyme and rhythm contributing to this end—while in the classical strophe the structure depends only on the rhyme, as each of its members conserves the rhythm individually.

This contributes, in turn, to rhyme's greater richness—and rhyme has replaced the strict rhythm of old verse as the essential element of modern verse.[8] With the increase in rhythmic variety, each strophe becomes further differentiated in the general tone of the composition.

Through an analogous adaptation as that which converted the melopoeia[9] of tragic choruses into the songs of our opera choruses, so melodic progress toward harmony characterizes the evolution of all Occidental music (and verse is music) until the classical strophe becomes the modern strophe: composed of unequal members combined at the will of the poet and subject to the supreme sanction of taste, as is everything in the fine arts.

The combinations produced in classical verses are very respectable, constituting as they do triumphant organisms in the selective process just described; but I repeat that they cannot pretend to be exclusive without clashing against the very same fundamentals of evolution that created them.

For this reason, the justification of any essay on free verse lies in the proper handling of excellently crafted classical verses, control over which determines the right to affect innovations upon them. This is a matter of basic honesty.

In addition to their intrinsic merit, classical forms persist by virtue of the law of the least effort. An ear accustomed to them in effect demands their continuing rule. But taken to its extreme, this phenomenon can lead to the triumph of the commonplace, which is to say to the degradation of language.

It is thus necessary to exalt the positive merits of free verse, so it may gain its natural citizenship among the others. There is nothing as effective toward this end as the use of varied and beautiful rhyme.

Note 8 states that rhyme is the essential element of modern verse. Our language possesses, in this regard, a great wealth. The Italian Petrarch is cited as an extraordinary case for having used five hundred and eleven different rhymes. We have more than six hundred usable ones available in Spanish.

And now, a couple of words of a personal nature.

Three years ago, when I announced that I was working on this book, I said: ". . . An entire book dedicated to the moon. A sort of vengeance of which I have dreamt almost since childhood, every time that I find myself overcome by life."

Could I have done it any better than allowing the obscure strength of the fight to spring from myself, so as to externalize the force in the shape of an excellent product, like the somber and noble sorrow that flows from the eyes distilled by crying crystal?

Is there a purer and more arduous enterprise in the world than that of singing to the moon to avenge life?

May it be worthy, then, of my Master Don Quixote, who counts the lunar body among his jewels for having defeated, in extraordinary battle, the Knight of the White Moon . . .

October 1909

The Ayacucho Address[1]

Ladies, Your Excellency the President of the Republic, Gentlemen:

Following the bronze hurricane just sounded by the epic bugles, preceded in turn by the noble silver horn with which the highest spirit in Colombia[2] has anticipated the acclamation, the Poet—owner and sire of his night of glory—has disposed that I am to close the march, if you will, by playing my hoarse retreat, on Maipo's old drum, to my heart's sincere beat.[3]

May this serve as an apology for the immense disadvantage of such a commission, as there is always something already withered in the laurel of the withdrawal.

Allow me, gentlemen, to say only that I shall endeavor to play my drum at the virile rhythm of your enthusiasm. And to you ladies, given that your presence here is my consolation, permit me to solicit—in the never disputed charity of your beautiful eyes, as one who hands an Argentine ribbon for a distinctive decoration, in the friendly symbol of white and blue—the favor of your grace and beauty.

Illustrious Captain of the Verb and Sire of Rhythm:

You have doubtlessly provided as a prologue to the Magnus Canto the only thing that properly corresponds to it: the voice of the earth in the uproar of the volcano; the voice of the air in the wind of the jungle; the murmuring voice of the water in the spattering of the waterfall.

And so I will pronounce the commentary that you have requested. I will speak of the Ayacucho that we see over there, in the fire alighting over the summits, whose word you have drawn by hammering the gold and iron of the sun of the Andes. And because the horror of vain words is the sweetest fruit that I have of a sour life, I shall try to elucidate the possible benefits that Ayacucho's lesson of the sword represents for man today.

Just as in the time of the Inca, when as a fair homage to the Son of the Sun the best of each natural element was brought as an offering from each country, the Republic of Argentina has now sent to Ayacucho's glorious Perú everything encompassed under the domain of its progress and its strength.

We thus had, firstly, the unforgettable emotion of that day when we saw appearing over Lima's dawning pearly sky the arrival of that strong youngster,[4] trailing along, attached to his airplane's vibrant wings, a pennant of Argentine sky.

We thus had the Argentine cannon of the battleship,[5] entering to the salute of the profound shots with which the heart of the homeland seemed to beat: slow, somber, formidable, the hull striped by the biting green sea, yet waving the greeting of the immense Río de la Plata in the smiling swirling of its flags.

We thus had the arrival of the armed forces, shining in the uniform of San Martín's grenadiers, and headed—if I may, with the permission of my general[6]—by the most competent, cleanest, and youngest sword of the Argentine command—of course without any disrespect to anyone else—bringing as homage the mountain of the condors and the pampa of the horsemen.

We thus had the intelligence of Argentina, arriving in the person of her most eminent practicians, and investing in me, not because of any particular merit, the charge of advancing the representation of the National Academy of Sciences of Córdoba, of the University of La Plata, of the Argentine Circle of Inventors, of the Circle of the Press, of the National Conservatory of Music, of the Association of the Friends of the Arts and of the National Counsel of Education, which in this manner presents to Perú the greeting of forty thousand teachers.

And finally, because it is my most precious right, because it constitutes my only personal asset, that Argentine goldfinch that sings that eternally young song of excitement and love in my heart.

It is thanks to him that I believe I know the heroic beauty of Ayacucho as if I had been there myself.

At the sound of forty reveilles the insurgent field awakens under the golden splendor and the sharp coolness of a morning of battle. The multicolor shine of the harnesses of the horses dazzles in the royal field of the Spaniards. In the patriot, the uniform's dark blue fabric dresses with monastic poverty the austerity of the republic. Barely are a pair of such epaulettes able to shine there in the sun. And with its danger-provoking scarlet stain, the unmatched shoulder cape of Laurencio Silva, the tremendous black lancer from Colombia.

But it is here that, following their noble inclination, reestablishing the customs of a gentleman's war, the officers of both armies unsheathe their swords prior to commencing battle and come to the middle ground to converse and say farewell. And so those who had been friends in other times and even blood brothers, who are also present, embrace there before the armies, without hiding their tender tears. And then Monet, the arrogant and sumptuous Spaniard, descends from the mountain, his chestnut-colored beard combed like a sunflower, to warn Córdova the Insurgent that the fighting is about to begin.[7]

The final clash is a model of nobility and bravery. Coordinated like a tournament, the victory directed with aesthetic precision by the young marshal, at once elegant and refined like a rapier, there was no day in the entire war bloodier than that battle—so bloody, in fact, that one quarter of the combatants fell in the first two hours of battle. While Córdova's division rushes forth to the sentimental melody of the *bambuco*,[8] the battalion from Caracas, awaiting its turn—which will be terrible indeed—plays under the bullets with the dice of death.

The patriots lack much artillery and soon lose that which they had to the royalists, whose cannons in the center dominate the valley. But as if he had real bronze colts, the battle to Sergeant Pontón[9] is nothing more than a quadruple charge of sables, lances, and bayonets.

A charge by Córdova, he of the celebrated voice of command, who, with sword held high, rushes forward, head elevated without helmet, the ancestry of Achilles curling into gold as the sun alights upon his bright red hair. A charge by Laurencio Silva,[10] who satiates his lance with the devastation of eight royalist squadrons. A charge by Lara, who closes the fence of death, burying the iron of the head of his lance into the heart of the enemy.

And here the last charge, the one that will decide the victory. They are the Peruvian Hussars from Junín, under the command of the Argentine Colonel Suárez.[11] And with them, at the order of Bruix,[12] the eighty last mounted grenadiers. Of the four thousand men who crossed the Andes with San Martín, they are the only ones left. Of these, most have already turned gray: their sables reduced by half by the persistent grinding that sharpens the blade all the way down to the sword guard. And at that instant, from the rear, from where the crown of the final episode will be provided, they spur their horses and advance. See them crossing the field, gaining on the tip of their own whirlwind. They are there now, they are already upon them. A flash, a bolt of lightning, a shout: *Long live the homeland! . . .* —and at a slash, spilled like roses of glory, the last blood of the soldiers of the king.

Those tears from Ayacucho will justify the memory of others that I dare mention now, encouraged by the cordiality of your reception.

And this is that other memory: a night from my youth, in my native mountain range, the adolescent that I was turned pale over the book that narrated the stories of Miguel Grau's vessel.[13] The adolescent experienced his soul expand with the accomplishments of the small monitor,[14] embellished even further by the fog of misfortune. And feeling a cry building in his throat, a flower of salt that seemed to exude with the bitterness of the distant sea, he spilled upon the bosom of the Argentine mountains, alone before the night and the eternal stars, the dark tears cried by the *Huáscar*.

Gentlemen: Allow me to attempt to show that this hour of emotion not be useless. For I would also like to assume a risk by saying something that is very difficult to say in these times of paradoxical freedom and failed, although bold, ideology.

Once again, for the good of the world, the hour of the sword has sounded.

Just as the sword has accomplished our only real achievement to date, which is to say, our independence, it will likewise now create the order that we need; it will implement that indispensable hierarchy that democracy has to this date ruined—which it has in fact fatally derailed, for the natural consequence of democracy is to drift toward demagogy or socialism. But we know too well what collectivism and peace have accomplished, from the Incas of Perú to the Mandarins of China.

Pacifism, collectivism, democracy: these are synonyms of the same vacancy that destiny offers the predestined chief—which is to say the man who rules by his right of being better, with or without the law. For the law, as an expression of potential, becomes confused with its will.

Pacifism is nothing other than the cult of fear, or a decoy of the Red conquest, which defines it, in turn, as a bourgeois prejudice. Glory and dignity are the twin daughters of risk; and even as the true male rests, the sleeping lion raises his ear.

A complete life is defined by four verbs of action: to love, to fight, to order, to teach. Notice that the first three, however, are but alternate expressions for conquest and strength. Life itself is a state of force. And since 1914 we owe this virile confrontation with reality once again to the sword.

In the conflict between authority and law—more frequent all the time, since it is a natural consequence—the man of the sword must align himself with the former of the two. Such are his duty and his sacrifice. The constitutional system of the nineteenth century has expired. The army is the last existing aristocracy, which is to say the last chance at hierarchical organization left before the demagogic dissolution. Only military life executes, at this moment in history, the superior life of beauty, hope, and strength.

Had I not said this, I would have betrayed the mandate of the swords of Ayacucho. For on this centenary, dear gentlemen, we celebrate the war of liberation; the triumph of the foundation of the homeland; the imposition of our will through the strength of our arms; the embellished death of that already divine rapture, which under its very last anguish feels its soul opening to the glory in the heroic rending of the scream of a bugle.

Poet and brother in arms, in hope and in beauty: that is what the hour of the sword can do.

Allow me to say to you Lima, and to you Perú, two final words directly from my soul.

Thank you, sweet city of smiles and roses. I render laurels to your fame, may they be of fine gold to parallel your homage, and palm trees to your beauty, which weakened—fortunate is he in his own submission—the Man of the Andes and created his stoicism. For who did not know for his own good—or his own bad—that the eyes of a girl from Lima were to cost him—no longer Hell, for they were given in sorrow—but the very security of Paradise? In the white of your clouds I see the sky flagged with the colors of my homeland, and in the tender blue the caress of a spreading Argentine gaze. And generously your smiles of friendship and your roses of gentility offer me the pearl of intimacy and the ruby of constancy.

And to you, nation of Ayacucho, land so argentine in its frankness and in its beauty;[15] homeland where I no longer feel a foreigner, my homeland of Perú: your bliss lives on into immortality, your hope lives on, your glory lives on.

On Immigration

from *The Great Argentina* (1930)

A comfortable life, a higher salary, an ease in obtaining one's own house, and thus obtaining nationality: these shall make immigration to our land desirable. Immigration is not an eccentric phenomenon; rather, it is a function of internal markets, which determine the parameters of immigration through remunerating demand and help it take root by providing permanent advantages. Since man is the main resource, an increase in population occasions increases in labor, production, and consumption, explaining the increase in the general welfare as the country becomes populated. Because public and private services increase proportionally, without a rise in their expenses, these services earn more and can better compensate the workers they need. More consumption, as I have already stated, lowers the price of goods, and the growing density of human population makes it easier to ensure that everyone has a comfortable and inexpensive life. Just look, for example, at the streetcars and buses of large cities. When the country's actions are attractive to man and, reciprocally, man's actions are productive for the country, its economic and social organizations can fulfill their objectives, which is the general well-being of all its citizens. Since immigration has been stopped for a few years now, our affairs have not gone well. Too slowly is the country being populated and hence too slowly does it progress. This is the case even in Buenos Aires, if one compares it to other large cities of the world.

Although our annual birthrate is maintained at an average of 33,000, which corresponds to the normal fecundity of the human species, the capital, home to over two million inhabitants, has a lower birthrate. Meanwhile, miscarriages and infant mortality rates are high almost everywhere in the interior of the republic. We need to attract immigration to populate ourselves, and this will occur if we properly organize our internal markets.

Organizing our markets will likewise allow us to meet two very important conditions: the selection of the elements that we are to incorporate, with attention paid to their productive efficacy and fecundity, and the correlative determination of its race. The "Johnson Law,"[1] in force in the United States since 1924, constitutes a valuable lesson, if ever there was one, of an expression of the greatest experiment of human concurrence carried out to this date.

Needless to say, we need to prevent a rushed and crowded congestion. Given the formation of the European mind and consciousness, which is simply the natural consequence of such events, every mass immigration is a movement of colonization. This is proven by the spiritual state revealed in

Rome by the Conference on Emigration, and by the law of double citizenship in force in Germany and incorporated into the current project of the Spanish constitution.[2] But all that will be ineffective if we know how to defend ourselves. We must therefore be able to install the immigrant in our land, while simultaneously disseminating with abundant publicity the conditions of this plan in the countries of origin, and even establishing economic and political agreements with the appropriate governments—for we all wish to avoid the transplantation of people predestined to misery from unemployment or incompetence. Such agreements, in addition to our own vigilance, will also prevent the damaging assembly of individuals whose antisocial character predisposes them to facile displacements. In every delinquent there is a fugitive, just as in every agitator there is an adventurer; and every Marxist or anarchist communist is an expatriate in his own country. They are elements of external disrepute for their motherland and of disturbance for ours: it is also very much in our common interest to prevent their entering our country. Likewise, it is in no way to our benefit to support a proletarian and adventurous immigration, as this overburdens our urban population and artificially increases the sectarian elements and the domestic services—the servile condition being itself parasitic and depressing. So much so, that this should constitute a legal impediment to obtaining citizenship. The profession of servant requires, in addition, sterility or abandonment of children; and these motives should suffice to limit the servile immigration, constituted primarily of women, which is to say by maternal wombs not utilized in this manner. The celibacy and conjugal fraud that such professional sterility imposes are, in turn, corruptive factors. Prostitution in the capital originates in large part from domestic servants. It is furthermore impossible to settle such a population, one that is permanently cruel and violent. A purely untrained immigration, therefore, does not benefit us; and just as in everything else, we must find the proper methodology. We must properly select and install the immigration so as to recast it as soon as possible into the national unity under which we are constituted.

The nation's digestive capacity, if you will, is excellent; and as a general rule, the first native generation belongs to us heart and soul. But it is just as true that national illegitimacy exists and that the heterogeneity of immigrant elements turns out to be disadvantageous. We can and we must, therefore, adopt preferences, not only concerning the economic capacity and the health and civic state of the immigrant, but also with regard to his ethnic character. And we must do so in accordance with this overarching concept: our country is not a refuge or a shelter, but an association of people living in agreement. No one has a right to turn our homeland into a source of charity, for if she is for everyone, she no longer belongs to anyone. Our homeland completely fulfills her mission when she suffices for her people. That is her reason for being and no other. The supreme goal of the homeland is to ascertain that her people are as happy and as strong as possible. Her morality demands that she not fulfill this goal at the cost of her own good.

To pretend that the homeland be host to all of humanity is a paradox that inverts to the point of the absurd the relationship between continent and content. Humanity is not a characteristic and responsible entity like the homeland. It is only the name of a species. Its constitution, if it can be articulated as such, is formulated by the rights of man. It is no more than, and cannot go beyond, this fact.

But such rights are not, nor can they be, political without in turn denying the homeland, which is a natural as well as a political reality. Thus, neither residency nor citizenship is a political right. For these are either native privileges, or ones bestowed in each homeland.

Bestowed for the good of the homeland and the one receiving residency, certainly; but above all, for the good of the homeland. The residence of a foreigner is therefore always a conditional state, and citizenship an honor with which he is distinguished. For this reason, too, the faculty of admission is discretionary and absolute. It never constitutes an obligation of the homeland, but only to herself.

The morality of the homeland demands that she not harm anyone but it does not force her to do good to anyone who is not her son. The homeland does not have obligations to humanity. Only man has such obligations. Humanity is not a group of homelands, because it is not a political being; it is rather, I repeat, a natural species. The ideology that confuses these notions is that of internationalism: a foolish illusion which, in the course of history, has failed more than once.

To make a homeland is to form an entity fit for a favorable life, one which can be improved—which is to say, an entity with a permanent, organic unity for the harmonic correspondence of its parts. And there is no greater destructive anarchy than the millenary conflict of the races.

The Republic of Argentina is not a condominium or an experimental colony of more or less prestigious ideologies. It belongs to Argentines, and only Argentines can administer her toward her stated goal. In proper accordance with all foreigners, while possible, and hopefully it always will be so. But never under the capitulation of the inadequate and the nonconformists.

We belong to the Latin race, and it is to our benefit that we do. Naturally, because we are. But also because, in this manner, we belong to the most noble of civilizations.

When Sarmiento pronounced that profound sentence, declaring that "we form an integral part of the Roman Empire," he formulated our true destiny with brilliant precision.

We must form a homeland with those people who are a benefit to us, not with those whom we may like for some sentimental or ideological satisfaction. We must not perform charity with our homeland, or philosophy with her destiny.

Nor is the labor of making a homeland defined only by present needs. It is also an effort nobly sacrificed for her future.

The Holiday of the Proletariat

article in *La montaña* (1897)

The Riffraff has its own Sundays. This is one of them. We are now so far from the old religion that we have had to create new holidays for ourselves. We do not have bells to inaugurate these days, nor flowers to adorn them, nor music to celebrate them. There is nothing sadder than the Sunday of an enslaved people.

But there is something immensely beautiful in this day of the oppressed: Hope.

Ragged, calloused, used, weakened, patched up, sick, we look like a bunch of rickety cages, seemingly with a lion inside each one. The lion is greatly pleased to see that his cage is rickety!

Hope! That is our Easter of Resurrection. Each one of us knows that he is trustee of a particle of dawn. He knows that, from his misery, vindication emerges like a threatening tree. He knows that something hurts him, and he does not want it to hurt. He knows that the chain's strength is measured by the degree of resignation of the victim who suffers with it.

Very well, then: this is why there is going to be a Revolution. We who suffer from the pain of servitude have proclaimed Liberty. We wish to tear down our jail, all of it! We want the social order, which is our jail, to disappear. And our aspiration extends from the granary to the academy.

Our protest is not just a matter of asking for bread, it is not just a group of hungry men. It is the outcry of protest against all slaveries, it is an opening of horizons for everyone's hopes. Being naked does not always mean being without clothes. We do not want to be naked!

The economy is, without a doubt, a major question, as it is the foundation of all social movements. We protest economic tyranny, we certainly protest economic tyranny, but other tyrannies exist as well. And we protest those other tyrannies, too. Which is why today, more than ever, the protest against the masters, carried out only by the servants, is so large: one might say that it is the future bringing the past to trial.

We protest the entire existing social order: that of the republic, the paradise of mediocrity and of the servile; that of religion, which chokes souls so as to pacify them (and how pacified they do in fact remain: never to move again!); that of the army, that cavern of slavery where the muzzle is worth more than the mouth, and where being a murderer and a thief is permitted in exchange for becoming an imbecile; that of the homeland, supremely false and evil, as the legitimate daughter of militarism; that of the state, which is a machinery of torture, under the pressure of which we must mold ourselves like chips in a house of games; that of the family, which is the pillar of the slavery of women and an inexhaustible source of prostitution. Against all of these capitalized bases of social convention, against all of these chains, we protest, we who are in chains.

And that is the real meaning of the movement that can be felt on this day on the faces of all the people; not only the vindication of a day of labor, but the war cry of the oppressed; not only the complaints of those in pain, but the threat of the strong; no longer the peaceful reasoning of the petitioners, but the imperious protest of the enemy; no longer the demonstration of the elements of labor, but the spectacle of the regiments of vindication; no longer the lyrical expression of a canon of justice, but the maximum program of the revolution.

And this is why it is as if the light of a lamp had been replaced by the sun. As if inside our lamp, instead of a wick, a star were now burning. We have put the wick away. The wick will be used for other purposes.

It is, thus, the Sunday of the Riffraff. And the demonstration of the event approaches, for the others do not know what day it is: they believe that it is the first of May of 1897.

Notes

The Rain of Fire

1. God destroys the Old Testament cities of Sodom and Gomorrah with a rain of fire and brimstone because of their sinfulness, allowing his follower, Lot, to escape with his family (Genesis 19: 17–26). (See "The Pillar of Salt" for another version.) Thus the names of Sodom and Gomorrah evoke apocalyptic images of divine punishment for transgression in Western consciousness.—Ed.

2. Here Lugones emphasizes Old Testament sources and God's implacable wrath with the epigraph from Leviticus and the reference to Sodom and Gomorrah from Genesis 19.—Ed.

3. An amphora is a two-handled vessel, of various shape, used by the ancients for holding wine, oil, etc.—Trans.

4. Asafetida is "the fetid gum resin of various Oriental plants (genus *Ferula*) of the carrot family, used in medicine as an antispasmodic" (*Webster's New Collegiate Dictionary* [1961]).—Ed.

5. Yellow orpiment is arsenic trisulphide, a bright yellow mineral that occurs naturally and was formerly used as a dye or artist's pigment. It is also called *yellow arsenic* and (as a pigment) *king's yellow*.—Trans.

6. Byssus is an exceedingly fine and valuable textile fiber and fabric known to the ancients; apparently the word was used, or misused, for various substances, such as linen, cotton, and silk, but it denoted properly (as shown by recent microscopic examinations of mummy cloths) a kind of flax, and hence is appropriately translated in the King James Bible as "fine linen."—Trans.

7. Natron is a native hydrous sodium carbonate, occurring chiefly in places like dried lake beds; any mineral salt containing this.—Trans.

8. Admah and Zeboim, along with Sodom, Gomorrah, and Zoar, constituted the "Five Cities of the Plain" (or Pentapolis), a rich and fertile region that now lies under the southern part of the Dead Sea. Various passages of the Old Testament refer to these cities, and speculation about their destruction has occupied historians, scientists, and religious scholars.—Ed.

Yzur

1. Dr. Paul Broca (1824–1880) was a French surgeon and pathologist and a founder of the discipline of anthropology, whose research on aphasia and the localization of the brain's speech areas was critically important. He developed instruments and methods for the study of craniology, the science that measured intellectual ability by brain size and capacity.—Ed.

2. Lugones refers to a number of scientists and, in doing this, reflects the concerns of his age with the interest in evolution and speech stimulated by Darwin's discoveries, leading to "scientific" theories of racial, gender, and species hierarchies. See also notes 19 through 23 of the introduction.—Ed.

3. Samuel Heinicke (Germany, 1727–1790) was a pioneer in deaf education, whose emphasis on the spoken word and lip-reading was in opposition to the practice of signing. Heinicke believed that speech is central to intellect, while other theorists contended that the sound production could be mere babbling, like that of a parrot.—Ed.

4. The procedure described in the story is logical—within the logic of Lugones's fiction, that is—for the teaching of Spanish, with the five distinct vowel sounds of Spanish. One would assume, however, that the

narrator's methods would be different if he were teaching Yzur a different language, such as English.—Trans.

5. One supposes—within the logic of the fictional narrative, of course—that this may have taken longer in English, which has more vowel sounds than Spanish.—Trans.

6. Quadrumana is an order of mammals, including monkeys, apes, baboons, and lemurs, of which the hind as well as the fore feet have an opposable digit, so that they can be used as hands.—Trans.

7. The phrase in Spanish the monkey utters is "AMO, AGUA, AMO, MI AMO." *Amo* in spanish means *master* and also as a conjugated verb it means *I love*. Thus there is a play on words with "master" and "love."—Ed.

Viola Acherontia

1. The title contains a reference to both plant and animal life, to the violet and to the Death's Head Moth (*Acherontia atropos*), on whose head can be seen skull-like markings. *Acherontia* comes from the name of the river (the Styx) that Charon ferried dead souls over to Hades.—Ed.

2. Jacques-Henri Bernardin de Saint-Pierre (1737–1814) was a French naturalist and writer whose works, including *Etudes de la nature* (1784), the widely read short novel *Paul et Virginie* (1788), and *La Chaumière indienne* [The Indian Cottage] (1790) stimulated the exaltation of nature in Western literature.—Ed.

3. The cotyledon is a leaf of the embryo of a seed plant, which upon germination either remains in the seed or emerges, enlarges, and becomes green. Also called seed leaf.—Trans.

4. Jules Michelet (1798–1874) was a French historian whose monumental works on French history, especially on the French Revolution, changed the nature of historical writing. His narratives sought to give an epic vision to French history and to celebrate Republican ideals. Like the Italian philosopher Giambattista Vico, he stressed the importance of human will in history and confronted the relation between violence and historical progress, insisting on the primacy of social and cultural, rather than political, institutions for understanding history.—Ed.

5. Jakob Friedrich Fríes (1773–1843), a German philosopher, sought to modify Kant's philosophy by emphasizing the subjective basis of consciousness and belief. He was attacked by Hegel for his relativism and anti-Semitic writings.—Ed.

6. John Gould (1804–1881) was a British ornithologist and artist who produced over three thousand bird drawings, including the fifty bird illustrations for Darwin's *The Zoology of the Voyage of the HMS Beagle* (1838–1943).—Ed.

7. The Swedish playwright August Strindberg (1849–1912) was also a painter and experimental photographer. In his essay, "The Death's Head Moth [acherontia atropos], an Experiment in Rational Mysticism" (1896), he likens the reflections from gelatinous fish scales to silver plate photography while arguing for the role of chance in species selection. Lugones was surely intrigued by the justification of the skull-like markings on the moth's head.—Ed.

8. See note 2. Lugones's abundant scientific and pseudo-scientific references point to his encyclopedic interests in many disciplines and highlight his era's preoccupation with the wonders and dangers of modern science and its effects on traditional society. While Lugones's erudite allusions may sometimes seem pedantic, in this story their cohesion and multilayered allusions combine to produce uncanny effects.—Ed.

9. Francis Bacon (1561–1626), an English philosopher and scientist, was a creator of the scientific method whose *Novum Organum* (1620) demolished scholastic methods.—Ed.

10. Toluidine blue is a thiazine dye, now used chiefly as a biological stain. Xylene is a mixture of three isomeric hydrocarbons obtained as a volatile colorless liquid from wood-spirit or coal-naphtha.—Trans.

11. A cissoid curve is a curve of the second order invented by Diocles, referred to as the *cissoid of Diocles.*—Trans.

The cusp of the cissoid resembles the re-entrant angles of the ivy leaf (*Oxford English Dictionary* [1971]).—Ed.

12. Solanine, daturine, ptomaine, leukomaine, belladonna, and stramonium are naturally occurring alkaloids that can be deadly poisonous. Belladonna and stramonium are also medicinally used for their narcotic or anti-spasmodic effects.—Ed.

13. Augustin-Pyramus de Candolle (Switzerland, 1778–1841) was the foremost botanist of his time. He was a founder of botanical geography and contested the classificatory system of Linnaeus.—Ed.

The Pillar of Salt

1. A terebinth tree is of moderate size, *Pistacia Terebinthus*, N.O. *Anacardiaceæ*, a native of Southern Europe, Northern Africa, and Western Asia, the source of Chian turpentine, and a common object of veneration; also called turpentine tree, and Algerine or Barbary mastic-tree. Apples of Sodom, or Dead Sea Fruit, are described by Josephus as of fair appearance externally, but dissolving, when grasped, into smoke and ashes; a "traveller's tale" supposed by some to refer to the fruit of *Solanum Sodomeum* (allied to the tomato), by others to the *Calotropis procera*, fig. It can also be any hollow, disappointing specious thing.—Trans.

2. Anchorites are persons who have withdrawn or secluded themselves from the world; usually for religious reasons; recluses, hermits.—Trans.

3. Cenobites are members of a religious order living in a community; opposed to an anchorite, who lives in solitude.—Trans.

4. Caesarea was an ancient seaport of Palestine south of present-day Haifa, Israel. It was founded (30 B.C.) by Herod the Great and later became the capital of Roman Judea. The city was destroyed by Muslims in 1265.—Ed.

5. In Genesis 19:17–26 God commands Lot and his family to flee Sodom before it is destroyed: "Escape thee for thy life; look not behind thee, neither stay thou in all the plain; escape to the mountain, lest thou be consumed" (19:17). But Lot's wife turns back to look: "But his wife looked back from behind him, and she became a pillar of salt" (19:26, King James version). Her transgression is looking at what is forbidden, and her punishment seals her secret. See also note 8 in "The Rain of Fire."—Ed.

6. Juvencus, an Iberian priest of the fourth century A.D., wrote epic verse (in four books of Latin hexameter) in the tradition of Homer and Virgil, but with Christ as the epic hero. Although Lugones attributes

the title to Juvencus, its source is more likely Sedulius, a fifth-century Christian Latin poet.—Ed.

7. Bitumen is, originally, a kind of mineral pitch found in Palestine and Babylon, used as mortar, etc. The same as asphalt, mineral pitch, Jew's pitch, *Bitumen judaicum* (*Oxford English Dictionary*).—Trans.

8. See note 5. The monk is asking her to divulge what she saw when she looked backward.

9. Elohim is one of the Hebrew names of God, or of the gods.—Trans.

The Escuerzo

1. An *escuerzo* is a kind of horned frog (*Ceratophrys ornate*), found primarily in the pampas of Argentina. In this story, Lugones also taps into the legends surrounding the *escuerzo* that exist in the gauchesque tradition.—Trans.

2. Batrachomyomachy is a mock heroic poem about a battle of frogs and mice, possibly of the Homeric age.—Trans.

3. *Mate* is a kind of herbal tea drunk widely in the region.—Ed.

The Horses of Abdera

1. Abdera, a city traditionally founded by Hercules on the spot in Thrace where Abderos was killed by Diomede's horses, was in fact colonized ca. 656 B.C. from Klazomenai. Refounded ca. 500 B.C. by refugees from a Persian occupation of Teos (southwest of Smyrna), it became a prominent member of the Delian League and famous for the beauty of its coinage. Democritus, the fifth-century philosopher who expounded an atomic theory; Protagoras (ca. 481–411), the first of the Sophists; and Anaxarchos, the counselor of Alexander the Great, were all born in Abdera.—Ed.

2. In Balastra on the Aegean Sea the ruins of the ancient town of Abdera may still be seen. They cover seven small hills.—Ed.

3. Lugones distinguishes the Thracian Abdera from the city named Abdera that existed in southern Spain (today Almería).—Ed.

4. The Ciconians, or Cicones, who lived on the southwestern coast of Thrace, sided with Troy against the Achaean invaders during the Trojan War. The Bisaltos (or Bisaltae) were the inhabitants of Bisaltas in Thrace.—Ed.

5. See note 6 in "The Rain of Fire."—Ed.

6. Arion was a fabulous horse begotten by Poseidon. Neptune, the Roman god of water and of the sea, derives from the Greek god Poseidon and incorporates his traits. Originally Poseidon was the god of horses and was worshipped in horse form. As creator of the horse, he was said to have taught men the art of managing horses with bridles.—Ed.

7. Podaros and Lampon are two of the four man-eating mares owned by Diomedes, king of the Bistones in Thrace. The eighth labor of Heracles was an order by the King of Argos to capture these wild mares. According to legend, Heracles took with him his lover Abderus, who in the fighting was eaten by the mares. Heracles then built the town of Abdera in his honor. The horses were said to be so bloodthirsty because they drank the water of the Kossinites River (today Kossynthos). These horse names appear as well in Homer and other sources, but in this case, Lugones is referring to the legend of the mares of Diomedes.—Ed.

8. See note 7.—Ed.

9. The Rhodope Mountains are a mountain range in present-day Bulgaria. The Nestos River rises in the Rhodope Mountains in Bulgaria and divides Macedonia geographically from Thrace.—Ed.

10. Pelasgians were people living in the region of the Aegean Sea before the coming of the Greeks. Pelasgian was, according to Mme. Blavatsky, the language that preceded the Vedic Sanskrit. (As was noted previously, Lugones had studied Blavatsky's writings.)—Ed.

11. A numen is a divinity, god; a local or presiding power or spirit.—Trans.

This Country's Politicians II

1. This was the second of a series of three articles Lugones published in 1897 in *La montaña,* this one on May 15.—Ed.

2. José Evaristo Uriburu became president of Argentina in 1895 when President Luis Sénz Peña resigned. Uriburu's presidency was noted for the strengthening of government institutions.—Ed.

3. A prebend is the stipend drawn from the Church for the support of the clergy. Here Lugones refers to state support.—Ed.

4. Luis Sáenz Peña (1822–1907) was president of Argentina from 1892 to 1895, during a period of economic depression and great social and political change resulting in part from increased European immigration. He repressed a rebellion by the emerging Radical Civic Union and was forced to cede the presidency to his vice president Uriburu in 1895. —Ed.

5. When Lugones died in 1938 he left an unfinished biography, *Roca*, of Julio Argentino Roca (1843–1914), who was president of Argentina from 1880 to 1886 and again from 1898 to 1904. As a military leader Roca gained renown in the Paraguayan War, but his leadership of the "Desert Campaign" (the conquest of Patagonia and indigenous groups) made him a national hero.—Ed.

6. Believers undertake annual pilgrimages to the National Basilica of Luján to pay homage to the Virgin of Luján.

The Morality of Art

1. A megathere is an extinct giant ground sloth; a megatherium.—Trans.

2. Neronian is a characteristic of the Roman emperor Nero (emperor A.D. 54–68); esp. tyrannical, extremely cruel, licentious.—Trans.

Prologue to the First Edition of Lunario Sentimental (Sentimental Lunarium)

1. Octosyllable verse is the most traditional form in Spanish and is associated with popular verse and song. While learned poets used other forms for several centuries, nineteenth-century poets like Bécquer (Spain) and José Martí (Cuba) reintroduced it precisely because of its popular and musical qualities.—Ed.

2. Lugones's abandonment of regular metrics in *Lunario Sentimental* shocked his contemporaries and sparked poetic experimentation in Spanish. Although he names this free verse, he did retain rhyme, and so today it would not be called free verse. See note 8 by Lugones.—Ed.

3. Cicero, *De Oratore*, book III. In the *Orator.* Cicero perceptively expands and formulates the aesthetics of oratory rhythm.

4. The *amphimacer* is a unit of prosody: "a trisyllabic metrical foot having an unaccented or short syllable between two accented or long syllables, as in *Peter Pan.* Also called *cretic*" (*American Heritage Dictionary*, 4th ed., 2000).—Ed.

5. Varro = Marcus Terentius (116–27 B.C.). Roman scholar and encyclopedist who reputedly produced more than six hundred volumes, covering nearly every field of knowledge. Cornelius Nepos (c. 100 B.C.–c. 25 B.C.), Roman historian. He was an intimate friend of Pomponius Atticus, Cicero, and Catullus. His only extant work is a collection of biographies, mostly from a lost larger work, *De viris illustribus* (On Illustrious Men).

6. Ricardo Jaimes Freyre (Bolivia, 1868–1933) was a major modernist writer and friend of Lugones. He is best known as the cofounder (with Rubén Darío) of the groundbreaking literary journal *Revista de América* (1894) and for his poems of *Castalia bárbara* (1918), poetry inspired by medieval Scandinavia. Lugones here refers to his essay "Laws of Spanish Versification" (1912, but published earlier in various journals), which emphasized the rhythmic basis of poetry in Spanish and its links with classical prosody.—Ed.

7. The verse form "romance" (roughly equivalent to "ballad" in English) is the oldest popular poetry in Spanish that originally was sung and not printed until the fifteenth century. Its origins are associated with national epic history although content is varied, and many *romances* survive today as part of oral tradition. The "romance" form consists of octosyllables with assonant rhyme (only vowels rhyme) in even verses with odd verses unrhymed.—Ed.

8. Well known is the structure of old verse, determined by the prosodic *quantity* of each syllable or foot: the combination of largos and breves producing a veritable music. Later, the quantity was no longer taken into account; rather, the verse was tuned in two or three syllables,

according to its accentuation, as we do now. Then rhyme substituted, with a more complex structure, for the musical effect that had been lost. It thus follows that rhyme is essential for modern verse. So-called rhymeless verses, denominated as *free* by the Spanish rhetoricians, are not, in effect, verses as such; and this is, above all, a rule for the hendecasyllable, although it is the one that is the most used in this manner; for no verse distances itself as much from the prosaic rules of old verse as the hendecasyllable does. This kind of liberty is but a recourse of impotence, for what is difficult in verse is rhyme—the essential element, as I have already stated, of the modern strophe. Richter, in his theories of aesthetics, has stated the following great truth: "The poet must renounce all that is easy, if there is no satisfactory explanation for using something easy; for such easiness is the easiness of prose." Varied, multiple rhymes determine in turn new modes of expression and enrich the language.

[Jean Paul Richter (Germany, 1763–1825), writer, published *School for Aesthetics* in 1804, which influenced Carlyle, DeQuincey, and Coleridge and constitutes an important document for romanticism.—Ed.]

9. Melopoeia is the art of composing melodies. It is also interesting to note that in ancient Greek theatre, melopoeia was the musical aspects and qualities of theatrical language and performance. It was also Ezra Pound's term for the musical and rhythmic qualities of poetic language, especially as suited to the tone or mood of the text.—Trans.

The Ayacucho Address

1. Lugones traveled to Ayacucho, Peru, to deliver this address at the anniversary of the Battle of Ayacucho, the final and decisive battle of the independence wars against Spain. Its belligerent tone and embrace of militarism sealed Lugones's reputation as antidemocratic, as had the speeches delivered the year before in Argentina.—Ed.

2. Don Guillermo Valencia, illustrious writer and chief of his country's extraordinary embassy.

3. The Battle of Maipo (1818) in Chile was an important victory for independence armies, led by Argentina's José de San Martín. With

Chile now independent, the revolutionary army then had strategic entrance into Peru.—Ed.

4. The aviator Hilcoat.

5. The *Moreno*, under the orders of Mr. Commandant Cueto.

6. Argentine Ambassador General Justo, minister of war.

7. In the decisive Battle of Ayacucho, General Córdova was a division commander under General José Antonio de Sucre, and General Monet was a division commander for the Spanish forces.—Ed.

8. *Bambuco* was a popular dance from Colombia.—Trans.

9. José Antonio Pontón was an officer from Ecuador who served with distinction under the command of General Sucre.—Ed.

10. Laurencio Silva was a Venezuelan general under the command of Sucre.—Ed.

11. The young Argentine Manuel Isidoro Suárez (Borges's great-grandfather on his mother's side) led the Peruvian and Colombian cavalry in the Battle of Junín. Suárez was hailed as a hero both in Junín and in Ayacucho. He was promoted to colonel by General Bolívar. Borges evokes him in the poems "Sepulchral Inscription" (*Buenos Aires Fever*, 1923), "A Page to Remember Colonel Suárez, Victor in Junín" (*The Other, The Self*, 1969), and "Colonel Suárez" (*The Iron Coin*, 1976).—Ed.

12. Under General Sucre, Colonel Alejo Bruix led the grenadiers against the Spanish forces of General Monet in Ayacucho.—Ed.

13. Miguel Grau (1834–1879) was a Peruvian naval officer. Grau commanded the *Huáscar* during the war with Chile, successfully sinking one Chilean ship and capturing another. The *Huáscar* was ultimately captured after a two-hour sea combat, but Grau remained a national hero.—Ed.

14. A monitor was an ironclad warship of the nineteenth century, having a very low free-board and one or more revolving turrets containing heavy guns.—Trans.

The ironclad *Huáscar* was the most important ship in Peru's nineteenth-century navy, in service from 1866. In the War of the Pacific the *Huáscar* defended Peru and attacked Chile's coasts and ships for many months against the formidable Chilean. Almost half of her two-hundred-man crew, including Grau, were killed during her last fight in 1879, an event that permitted the Chileans to invade Peru.—Ed.

15. There is a play on words here. In the original ("Y tú, nación de Ayacucho, tierra tan argentina por lo franca y por lo hermosa . . ."), when Lugones names the "nation of Ayacucho" as being "argentine," there is a double implication: "argentine" as in silvery, and "Argentine" as in his own homeland. (In Spanish, *argentino* as an adjective is not capitalized, whether it means silvery or someone or something from Argentina.)—Trans.

On Immigration

1. The Johnson-Reed Act of 1924 significantly altered immigration policy in the United States. Fears concerning the massive immigration from southern and eastern Europe (especially of Jews) and from Asia changed immigration policy. The act initiated a quota system from each country, thus limiting immigration from certain regions. This system was in effect until 1965.—Ed.

2. In 1924 an international conference on emigration and immigration was held in Rome to address the legal, political, and social issues resulting from increased international migration. Several countries were adjusting their citizenship requirements to allow emigrants to retain their original citizenship even as they acquired citizenship in their new countries. German laws of 1914 permitted dual citizenship, and the Spanish Constitution of 1931 officially allowed dual citizenship. Here Lugones alludes to divided loyalties among new immigrants to Argentina.—Ed.

Bibliography

Altamirano, Carlos, and Beatriz Sarlo. "La Argentina del Centenario: Campo intelectual, vida literaria, y temas ideológicos." *Ensayos argentinos: De Sarmiento a la vanguardia*, ed. Altamirano and Sarlo. Buenos Aires: Centro Editor de América Latina, 1983, 69–106.

Ara, Guillermo. *Leopoldo Lugones*. Buenos Aires: Editorial Mandrágora, 1958.

Barcia, Pedro Luis. "Los cuentos desconocidos de Leopoldo Lugones." LL., *Cuentos desconocidos*. Buenos Aires: Ediciones del 80, 1982, 7–52.

———. "Lugones y el ultraísmo." In *Estudios literarios*. La Plata: Universidad Nacional de la Plata, Facultad de Humanidades y Ciencias de la Educación, 1966.

Borges, Jorge Luis. *Leopoldo Lugones*. Buenos Aires: Troquel, 1955.

Canedo, Alfredo. *Aspectos del pensamiento político de Leopoldo Lugones*. Buenos Aires: Ediciones Marcos, 1974.

Capdevila, Arturo. *Lugones*. Buenos Aires: Aguilar Argentina, 1973.

Corvalán, Octavio Electro. "La madurez de Leopoldo Lugones." Ph.D. diss., Yale University, 1971.

Cúneo, Dardo. *Leopoldo Lugones.* Buenos Aires: Editorial Jorge Alvarez, 1968.

Dabove, Juan Pablo. *Nightmares of the Lettered City: Banditry and Literature in Latin America 1816–1929.* Pittsburgh: University of Pittsburgh Press, 2007.

Darío, Rubén. *Escritos inéditos de Rubén Darío,* ed. E. K. Mapes. New York: Instituto de las Españas, 1938.

Echagüe, Juan Pablo. *Seis figuras del Plata.* Buenos Aires: Editorial Losada, 1938.

Fraser, Howard M. *In the Presence of Mystery: Modernist Fiction and the Occult.* Chapel Hill: North Carolina Studies in the Romance Languages and Literatures. UNC Department of Romance Languages, 1992.

Ghiano, Juan Carlos. *Lugones escritor. Notas para un análisis estilístico.* Buenos Aires: Editorial Raigal, 1955.

———. *Temas y aptitudes (Lugones, Güiraldes, Quiroga, Arlt, Marechal, Bernárdez, Borges, Molina).* Buenos Aires: Ollantay, 1949.

Giusti, Roberto F. "Lugones helenista." *Nosotros,* año X, tomo 22, no. 84 (mayo 1916), 180–83.

González, Aníbal. "La escritura modernista y la filología." *Cuadernos Americanos* (México) (noviembre–diciembre 1981), 90–106.

———. *Journalism and the Development of Spanish American Narrative.* Cambridge: Cambridge University Press, 1993.

Halperín Donghi, Tulio. *Contemporary History of Latin America,* tr. John C. Chasteen. Durham, N.C.: Duke University Press, 1993.

Henríquez-Ureña, Max. *Breve historia del modernismo.* México: Fondo de Cultura Económica, 1954.

———. *El retorno de los galeones y otros ensayos.* 2nd ed. México: Ediciones Galaxia, 1963.

Hernández, Juan José. "El signo prohibido de Leopoldo Lugones." Suplemento "Cultura" del diario *Tiempo Argentino* (15 enero 1984), 1–3.

Irazusta, Julio. *Genio y figura de Leopoldo Lugones.* Buenos Aires: EUDEBA, 1968.

Jitrik, Noé. *Las contradicciones del modernismo.* México: El Colegio de México, 1978.

————. *Leopoldo Lugones: Mito nacional*. Buenos Aires: Ediciones Palestra, 1960.

————. *The Noé Jitrik Reader*, ed. Daniel Balderston, tr. Susan Benner. Durham, N.C.: Duke University Press, 2005.

Kirkpatrick, Gwen. *The Dissonant Legacy of Modernismo: Lugones, Herrera y Reissig, and the Voices of Modern Spanish American Poetry*. Berkeley: University of California Press, 1989.

Lermón, Miguel. *Contribución a la bibliografía de Leopoldo Lugones*. Buenos Aires: Ediciones Maru, 1969.

Ludmer, Josefina. *The Corpus Delicti: A Manual of Argentine Fictions*, tr. Glen S. Close. Pittsburgh: University of Pittsburgh Press, 2004.

————. *The Gaucho Genre: A Treatise on the Motherland*, tr. Molly Wiegel. Durham, N.C.: Duke University Press, 2002.

Lugones, Leopoldo. *Cuentos desconocidos*, ed. Pedro Luis Barcia. Buenos Aires: Ediciones del 80, 1982.

————. *Obras en prosa*. Madrid: Aguilar, 1962.

————. *Obras poéticas completas*. Madrid: Aguilar, 1959.

————. *Las primeras letras de Leopoldo Lugones*. Buenos Aires: Ediciones Centurión, 1963.

Lugones, Leopoldo, hijo. *Mi padre: Biografía de Leopoldo Lugones*. Buenos Aires: Ediciones Centurión, 1949.

Magis, Carlos Horacio. *La poesía de Leopoldo Lugones*. México: Ediciones Ateneo, 1960.

Martínez-Estrada, Ezequiel. *Leopoldo Lugones: Retrato sin tocar*. Buenos Aires: Emecé Editores, 1968.

Mastronardi, Carlos. *Formas de la realidad nacional*. 2nd ed. Buenos Aires: Editorial Ser, 1964.

Monteleone, Jorge. "Lugones, canto natal del héroe." In *Yrigoyen entre Borges y Arlt (1916–1930)*, ed. Graciela Montaldo, vol. 7 of *Historia social de la literatura argentina*, ed. David Viñas. Buenos Aires: Contrapunto, 1989, 161–80.

Murena, H. A. "Ser y no ser de la cultura latinoamericana." In *Expresión del pensamiento contemporáneo*. Buenos Aires: Sur, 1965.

Nosotros (Número extraordinario dedicado a Leopoldo Lugones). Segunda Epoca, año II, tomo VII, no. 26–28 (mayo–julio 1938).

Nouzeilles, Gabriela. *Ficciones somáticas: Naturalismo, nacionalismo y políticas médicas del cuerpo (Argentina 1880–1910)*. Buenos Aires: Beatriz Viterbo, 2000.

———. "The Transcultural Mirror of Science." In *Literary Cultures of Latin America*, vol. 3, ed. Mario J. Valdés and Djelal Kadir. Oxford: Oxford University Press, 2004, 284–99.

Obligado, Carlos. "La vida y la obra de Lugones." In *Obras poéticas completas de Leopoldo Lugones*. Madrid: Aguilar, 1959, 13–47.

Omil, Alba. *Leopoldo Lugones: Poesía y prosa*. Buenos Aires: Minor Nova, 1968.

Payró, Roberto J. "El mercado de libros." *La Revista Nacional*, año II, no. 24 (16 junio 1895), 341–42.

Paz, Octavio. *Cuadrivio*. México: Joaquín Mortiz, 1969.

Pérsico, Adriana. "The Rhetoric of Citizenship in Modernity." In *Literary Cultures of Latin America*, vol. 1, ed. Mario J. Valdés and Djelal Kadir. Oxford: Oxford University Press, 2004, 384–400.

Pío del Coro, Gaspar. *El mundo fantástico de Leopoldo Lugones*. Córdoba: Universidad Nacional de Córdoba, 1971.

Rama, Angel. *The Lettered City*, tr. John Charles Chasteen. Durham, N.C.: Duke University Press, 1996.

———. *Las máscaras democráticas del modernismo*. Montevideo: Fundación Angel Rama, 1985.

Rivera, Jorge, ed. "Dossier Lugones." *Crisis* 14 (1974).

Rock, David. *Authoritarian Argentina: The Nationalist Movement, Its History, and Its Impact*. Berkeley: University of California Press, 1993.

Roggiano, Alfredo. "Bibliografía de y sobre Leopoldo Lugones." *Revista iberoamericana*, no. 53 (enero–junio 1962), 155–213.

Salessi, Jorge. *Médicos, maleantes y maricas: Higiene, criminología y homosexualidad en la construcción de la Nación Argentina (Buenos Aires 1871–1914)*. Rosario: Beatriz Viterbo, 1995.

Scari, Roberto Mario. "El idealismo del joven Lugones." *Cuadernos Americanos*, vol. 218, no. 3 (mayo–junio 1978), 237–48.

———. "La formación literaria de Lugones." Ph.D. diss., University of California, Berkeley, 1963.

Shumway, Nicolas. *The Invention of Argentina*. Berkeley: University of California Press, 1991.

Stepan, Nancy. *The Hour of Eugenics: Race, Gender and Nation in Latin America*. Ithaca, N.Y.: Cornell University Press, 1991.

Viñas, David. *Literatura argentina y realidad política*. Buenos Aires: Capítulos (Centro Editor de América Latina), 1982.

Yurkiévich, Saúl. *Celebración del modernismo*. Barcelona: Tusquets Editor, 1976.